How to
Sell
Seed Garlic
on the
Internet

How to Sell Seed Garlic on the Internet

Do-it-yourself
E-commerce Guide

Richard C. Harrison

Published by
Marbleharbor Press
3B Cliff Street
Marblehead, MA 01945

Google and the Google logo are registered trademarks of Google, Inc., used with permission.

Screen shots used by permission of:
Google Adwords™
Weebly®
PayPal®

ISBN-13: 978-0692532058 (Marbleharbor Press)
ISBN-10: 0692532056

Contents

Why this guide?

When I started selling seed garlic on the Internet I was not sure where to start. I investigated several larger scale e-commerce vendors and actually signed up for a short time with one, a large off-shore vendor with many good references. Although the system was impressive, I found that their website creation tool was not as simple as using Weebly. I had set up several non-e-commerce websites using Weebly so decided to try it for e-commerce.

Weebly e-commerce provides a shopping cart for purchases but needs to interface to an e-commerce check-out vendor to complete the credit card aspects of the transaction. Which of several vendors to choose? Since I needed to fulfill orders and Paypal provided a nice fulfillment option I chose to go with Paypal. Fulfillment support was not included in the large off-shore vendor noted above so I was able to select a check-out vendor and accomplish fulfillment with a single choice.

Finally, I needed to market my product. Google Adwords provided an ideal vehicle for my prospective customers to find me on the Internet. Since my average sale was around eighty dollars I could afford to use Google.

So, now that I had figured out which systems to use I had to learn how to use them. The learning curve, in spite of the rather extensive help systems provided, was rather stiff. So, the purpose of this book is to save you time. By reading my documentation on how I sold out my crop of seed garlic in five weeks, you can learn how to sell your own crop and save time to boot. So read on if this approach sounds appealing.

2

How to Sell Seed Garlic on the Internet: Overview

Like the three legs of a stool, e-commerce requires three primary functions: marketing, selling and fulfilling orders. In attempting to implement a simple e-commerce selling system for seed garlic, I found that e-commerce vendors seemed to understand the marketing and selling aspects of the problem but completely dropped the ball when it came to fulfillment.

The problem that I was attempting to solve seemed simple. Our customer would locate our site using a Google Internet search, order several types and pound sizes of garlic from our 15 varieties, and we would pick and ship the items ordered.

```
   Market                    Sell                  Fulfill

  ┌──────────┐          ┌──────────┐          ┌──────────┐
  │ Google   │          │ Weebly   │◄────────►│ PayPal   │
  │ Adwords  │          │          │          │          │
  └──────────┘          └──────────┘          └──────────┘
        ▲                    ▲▼                     ▲
         ╲              ┌──────────┐              ╱
          ╲            │ Customer  │◄────────────
           ─────────► └──────────┘
```

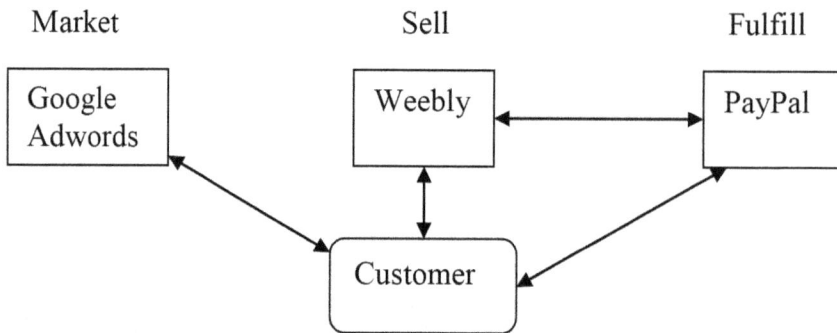

While the above process may appear to you to flow according to common sense, I found it nearly impossible to find a single affordable e-commerce system that performed these functions. What I will describe in this guide, *How to Sell Seed Garlic on the Internet*, will show you how we implemented a three-prong effective e-commerce system at a nominal cost. The three prongs of our e-commerce tool are: Google Adwords for marketing; Weebly Professional E-commerce for selling the product, a shopping cart, and PayPal for processing the e-commerce charges, generating the packing slip (also used for order picking) and printing the prepaid shipping labels. Using this combination we were able to sell out our garlic crop in five weeks in 2014.

Weebly

Weebly interfaces with Paypal which prepares the packing slip (picking form). In 2015 we will bag the orders in half pound, 1 pound, 5 pound or 10 pound bags as they are received using the packing slip. The packing slip is placed in the box, the box sealed, a prepaid label affixed to the top and the box shipped.

Although the process of an e-commerce system is Market > Sell > Fulfill, I will discuss the process in the order that I found easiest to understand. I started with a Weebly E-Commerce website. I had used Weebly before to create a website for our farm and had found it extremely easy to navigate. Weebly has a simple process of What-You-See-Is-What-You-Get editing and publishing of one's website. The navigation between pages on their edit site works almost identically to the navigation on your *finished* pages on the web. So one can up-load pictures and key in text easily and not get lost in the details.

Weebly e-commerce takes a bit of getting used to. First, they provide the format for listing your products. You, as author, need to upload pictures of your products, assign SKU's, descriptions, list prices, sale prices and product op-tions. All this is documented by Weebly on their site. Second, the Weebly ver-sion of your website, in edit mode, becomes your administrative access to your e-commerce system. In addition to tracking sales and allowing downloads of orders from the Weebly site, the full $300 e-commerce version allows you to input inventory. I found the inventory system to be very accurate, and I never had the situation of a back order due to an inventory error. It is important to remember to *publish* the website each time you visit it for management infor-mation so that any change that you make is stored. Of course, I checked the inventory carefully every day to make sure the physical inventory matched the database inventory on-line. This is not always practical for larger businesses. Finally, the Weebly system allows you to track orders, coding them as shipped, and gives you an ability to notify the customer that the order is on the way.

Shipping in Weebly E-Commerce may be done based on dollar value of the order or by weight. By far the easiest way to set up shipping is by dollar value. For 2015 we will use the dollar value table that we adopted from a leading seed producer with only 6 shipping rates. I attempted to use the weight method in 2014 and found it overwhelming; sometimes overcharging and sometimes undercharging for shipping. It is up to you as user to input the various shipping costs by distance and weight. We ended up using the US Postal Service fixed rate packages for longer distance 5 and 10 pound shipments, and lower rates for smaller shipments closer to our shipping location. For shipments over 20 pounds I used UPS, charging the max USPS rates initially and then refunding the customer for the difference between the max and the UPS rates. It is feasible to input UPS rates; however I didn't have time to do the research. Use the dollar value if you possibly can.

Weebly charges a fixed rate of $300 per year for their full e-commerce system which includes a nice shopping cart and interface to PayPal which I discuss below. In the event that your gross billings are under $10,000 per year, you have the option to select a Weebly a la carte system of 3% of each transaction. This is an affordable way to get going, however with the 3% plan you won't get the inventory control feature nor can you sell electronic downloadable products.

We bag and pick each product individually, label it with the variety and pounds, mark it with the name of the customer, and gather all the components of the order at the end of the picking process, compare to the packing slip for accuracy box up and ship the order. The packing slip and prepaid box label are printed via PayPal as discussed below.

PayPal

We specified PayPal as our e-commerce payment vendor. This is done within the context of Weebly. Thus, after the customer finishes ordering the items on the site having placed them in the shopping cart, when they *check out* they are taken to the PayPal site. If they are not registered with PayPal they may register on the spot, or if they don't care to register they can simply input their credit card data. PayPal is very secure. You, as vendor, never see the customer's credit card information. PayPal takes all credit cards. Once the order is placed in PayPal you will get an email from both the Weebly site and PayPal. By printing the email one can create a manual tickler file of all open orders, very handy for the smaller business. Of course the orders are also available on-line in both Weebly and PayPal with their order status. It is also possible to download the orders from both sites. The format of the download data is included in Appendix 1.0 for Weebly and Appendix 2.0 for PayPal.

Order Data

The order *detail* is available only on Weebly. In the PayPal download the charges are summarized for your gross billing. The PayPal fee and the fee for postage are all included.

Shipping Document (Packing Slip) and Prepaid Shipping Label

The Shipping Document (Packing Slip) that summarizes the complete order is produced from the PayPal system. It shows all line items ordered. When you log into PayPal, a dashboard is displayed that summarizes your account activity. Based on a date range, which you submit, all of your orders for that period will be displayed. You may download the data for the submitted date range as well. When you select an order you are given an option to print a Packing Slip and also a Prepaid Mailing Label. The complete status of the order is kept current, for example, if it has been shipped; the shipping cost and any refunds which may have been applied to the order are showing. Postage paid by the customer for shipping is charged under the Weebly system, and the actual postage paid by you, the vendor, is paid under the PayPal system.

3

Our Order Process

The flow chart below outlines our e-commerce process; each of the numbered nodes, 1 – 8, are discussed in detail. We include hints that we found helpful in facilitating the creation of our system rather than simply reproducing vendor documentation. We use screen shots to show you most of the steps necessary to set up your e-commerce system.

Seed Garlic Order Process Flow Chart

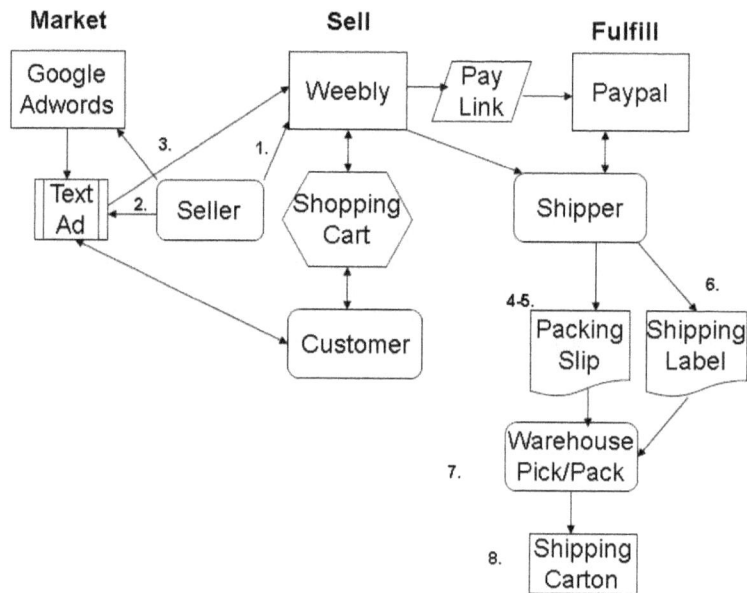

Creation of Weebly website (Node 1)

We created our website, www.OrganicMaineGarlic.com using Weebly, and recommend this process:

Try a couple of Weebly tutorials

If you have never developed a website using Weebly, I suggest that you read **A Beginners Guide to Weebly** found in the Weebly Help Center. The text includes some You Tube videos.

Weebly Template

In Weebly you need to pick a template. We picked the *Hands Planting* template noted below. As you scan down the templates you can find it toward the end. The reason we picked that template is the simple structure – a logo band across the top replacing whatever was there with our own logo, a single line menu bar with dropdowns, a short header (hands planting replaced with our own picture) where the topic of the screen is placed. Below the short header is the content including text and pictures. Constraints that we used to keep things simple are: 1) no more items on the top level menu bar than can be fit. This means that if you get into an overflow situation it is best to shorten up the menu text so everything fits on one line. 2) dropdowns, in general, only one level deep. Again this makes for a simple easy-to-navigate site. 3) use only text and pictures. Other stuff can wait.

Our approach is to implement only a fraction of Weebly's website capability using only what is absolutely necessary to get the message across and sell the product. Another benefit of a simple structure is that it is much easier to navigate on a smart phone or tablet. Weebly automatically gives you this latter capability.

Our e-commerce site, www.organicmainegarlic.com, will illustrate.

This is what our starter site looked like in the Theme pages.

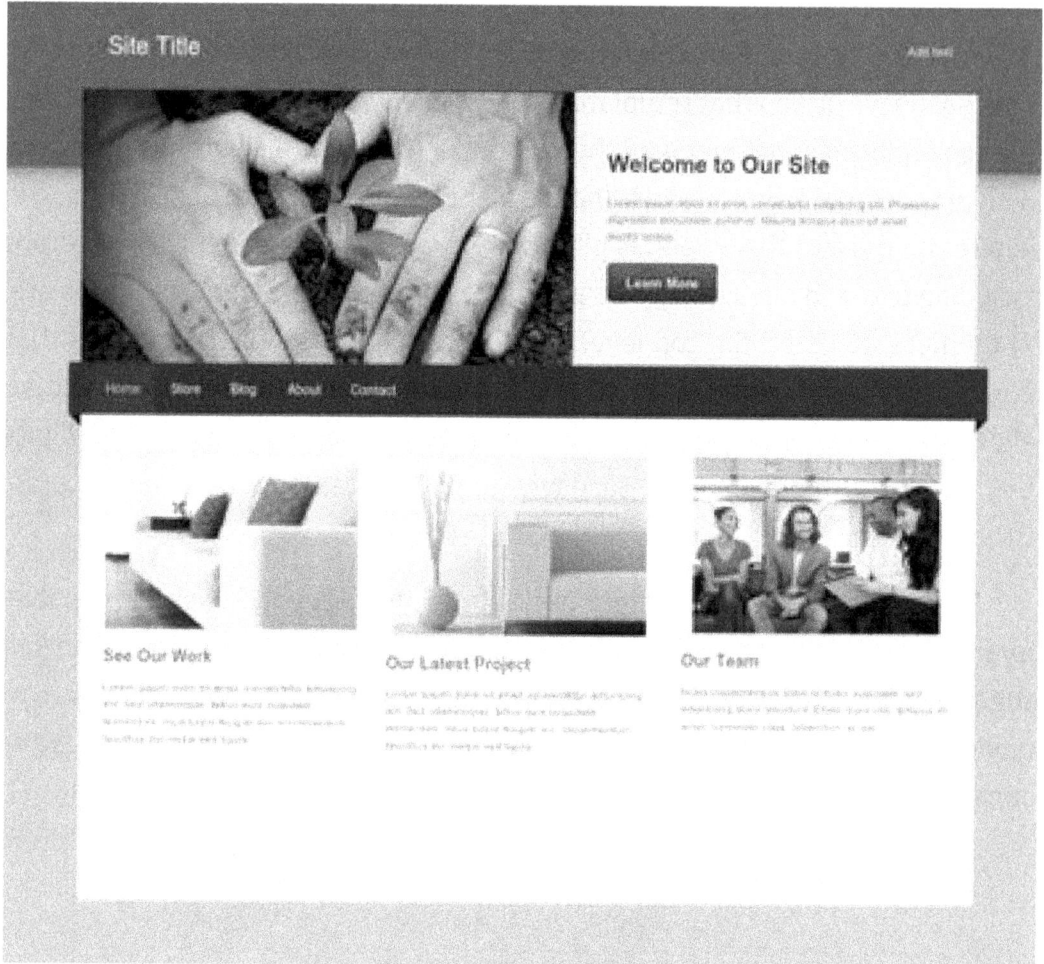

Once loaded, we modified so the homepage looks like this –

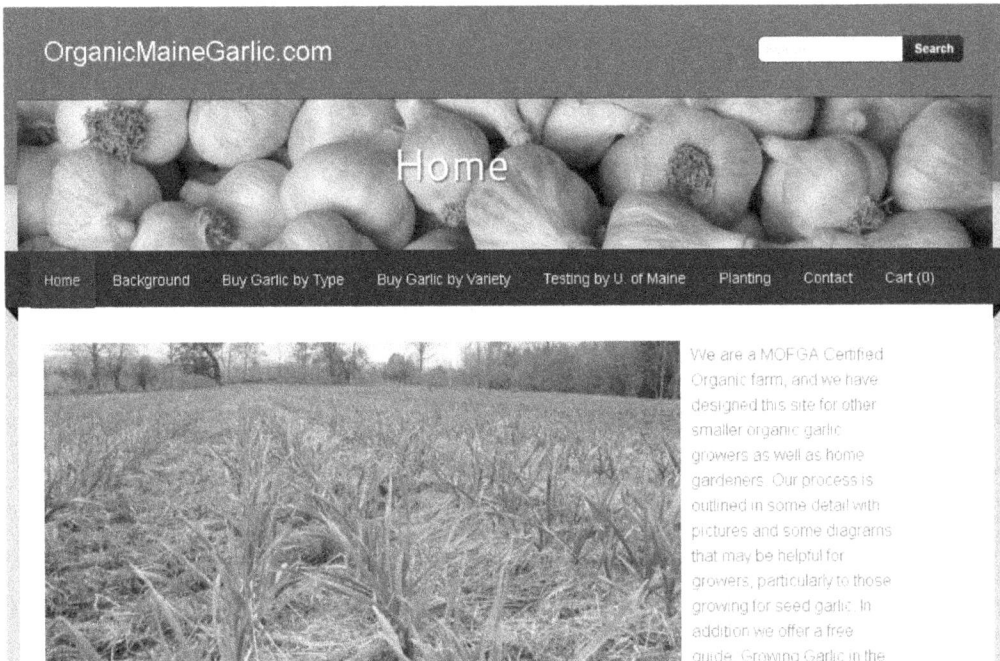

To change the very top section, the *logo* area of the pages, you mouse over the starter text, in the Hands Planting case, the words, Site Title. If Site Title doesn't appear mouse over the area and you will see the words, Off Text Logo. If you click on Text you can input the name of your site or any other standard header text to be used across all site screens. If you click Logo, you can upload a JPEG image, either a graphic or a picture from your computer that will then appear just above the menu bar shown below with the word Home.

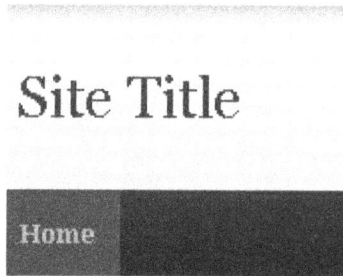

Next you can change the header area. In Build Mode, click on Edit Image and you will see the following screen. We used the Short Header on all our pages as a standard. You can choose Tall Header or No Header. You can upload a photo to replace the hands. The photo area may be larger than the Short Header area but Weebly will compensate for that. You should position the photo so that the Short Header displays what you want. When you get the photo in the right position you must Save. Indicate if you want to save to All Pages, This Page Only or to Selected Pages. You can also add text to the image. This is where we place our screen titles. In general we use the same Short Header throughout the site but save the text for each screen for *This Page Only.*

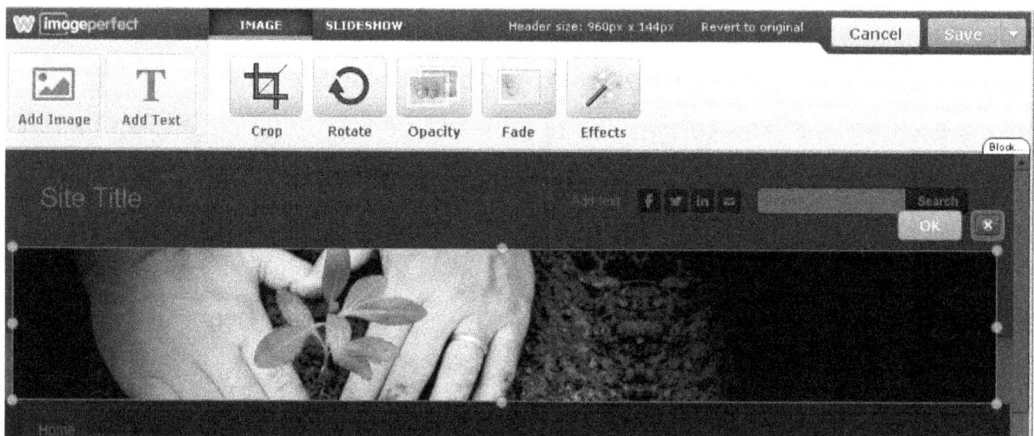

Finally we input text and a picture in the body of the page. Since we are keeping the website ultra-simple we usually show only one picture and some simple text. Use the Build Mode in order to enter material onto the body of the screen. For example:

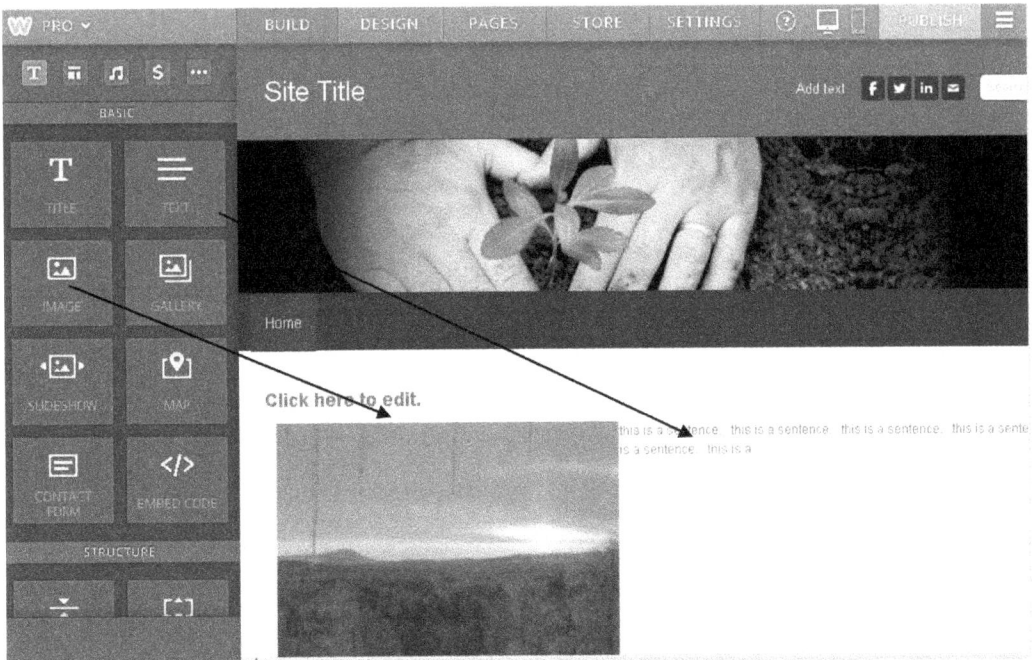

Simply drag the icon over the page and drop it to provide a text box for inputting text. When you drag the Image icon over the page you will be prompted to input a picture.

Weebly Menus

The Weebly menus are used to gain access to functionality on the top tabs.

BUILD – As mentioned above, the BUILD options are used to construct the individual website screens.

DESIGN – Used to change the overall options for the site such as the theme. Because a theme change can dramatically alter the look of your site we don't recommend making such an alteration once you have a considerable investment in the creation of web pages.

PAGES – Allows you to construct the hierarchy of screens. The title of each screen is input as well as the type and general format.

STORE – Used to construct the e-commerce options.

SETTINGS – Used to create and maintain the overall settings for the site.

E-Commerce

For each garlic variety that you are selling, you need to create a Product record. The example below will show one item in our garlic inventory that had three variations. All of the material entered onto the Product screen is redisplayed on the Product page that the customer sees. The Product Page for the variety shown is displayed below the Edit Product display.

Edit Product ⑦

View Product   + Copy Existing

Product Name

German Porcelain

Short Description

Easy to peel cloves. Best taste without too much heat and good storage. This variety does well in northern climate.

2014 Average: 8 bulbs per pound, 4 cloves per bulb

☑ Track Inventory ⑦   ☐ Charge Sales Tax ⑦

Product Images   + Add Images

Product SKUs (3) ⑦

Edit Options

Seed Garlic	Price	Sale Price	Weight	SKU	Inventory
Half Pound Bag	$ 12.00	$ 10.00	0.50 lb	GermanPorcelain .5	0
One Pound Bag	$ 20....	$ 18.00	1.00 lb	GermanPorcelain 1.0	0
Five Pound Bag	$ 80....	$ 75.00	5.00 lb	GermanPorcelain 5.0	0

+ Add SKU

Delete Product   ☐ Hidden ⑦   ☑ Storefront ⑦   Cancel   Save Product

One Edit Product page must be created for each of your products. The Edit Options button allows you to create a variation on the overall product; in our case, three bag sizes: Half Pound, One Pound and Five Pounds. These pages are for administrative purposes only and never appear to the customer. This is what the customer sees based on what you input on the Edit Product page.

E-Commerce Administration

One of the unusual things about Weebly is that your development site will also be your e-commerce administrative site. This means that each time you change anything with regard to the administration of your site you will need to *Publish* the website. You must publish even if you made no change to your website content, because you made changes to your administrative content. The screens below will illustrate.

When you click on STORE and then on Products, the software will take you to the following screen that shows you a list of all your products.

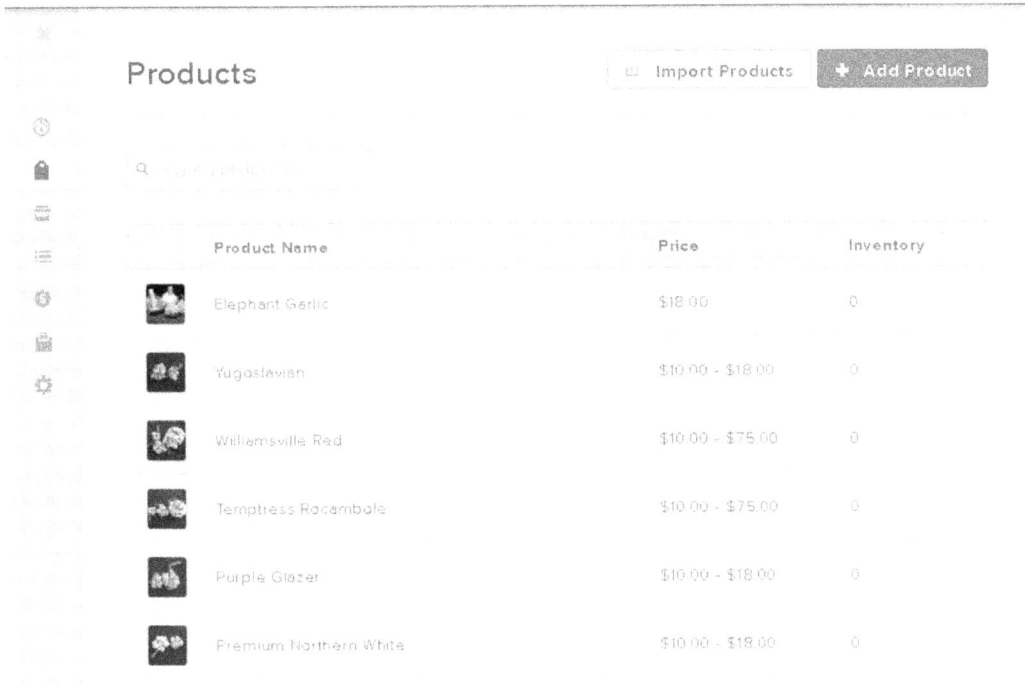

Products

Import Products   **+ Add Product**

Product Name	Price	Inventory
Elephant Garlic	$18.00	0
Yugoslavian	$10.00 - $18.00	0
Williamsville Red	$10.00 - $75.00	0
Temptress Rocambole	$10.00 - $75.00	0
Purple Glazer	$10.00 - $18.00	0
Premium Northern White	$10.00 - $18.00	0

The icons down the left hand side of the page allow you to navigate within the e-commerce administrative pages as follows;

	Dashboard – Summary of Orders
	Products – Overview of products

	Storefront – Product Table of Contents
	Categories – Grouping of Products
	Coupons – Checkout Discounts

	Orders -
	Settings – Overall

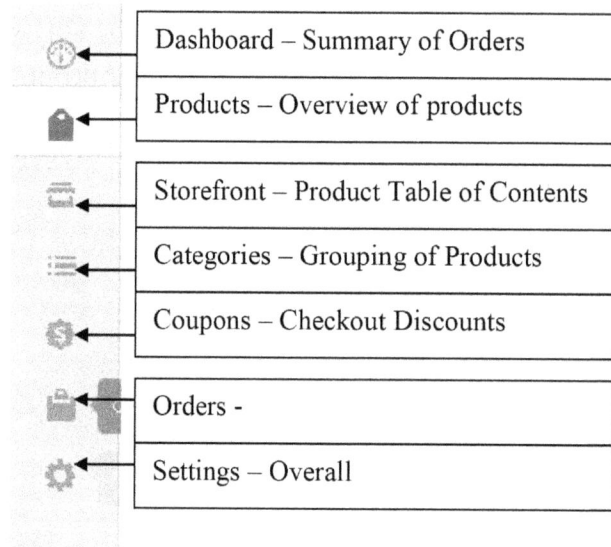

Settings in the Main Administrative Menu takes you to the sub-menu below -

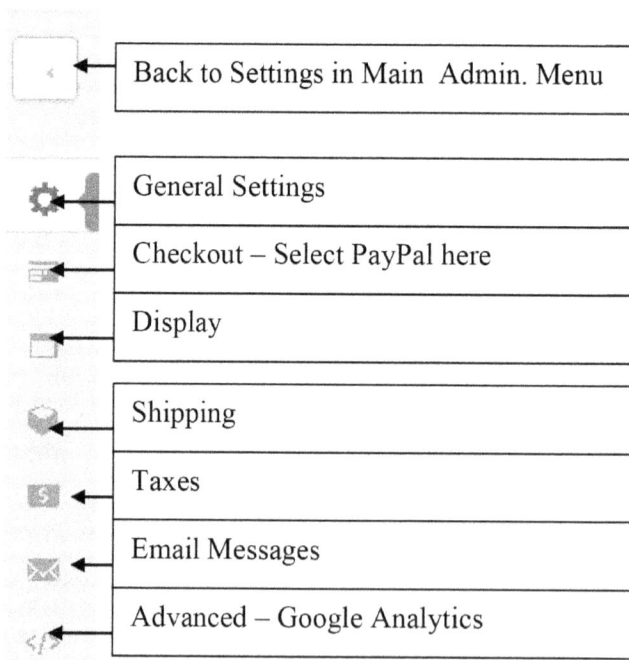

	Back to Settings in Main Admin. Menu

	General Settings
	Checkout – Select PayPal here
	Display

	Shipping
	Taxes
	Email Messages
	Advanced – Google Analytics

Noted on the screens that follow are examples of each of the selected options we used with www.organicmainegarlic.com. We didn't use all the options with that site; so in those cases I show the Weebly unfilled forms.

Dashboard Summary of Orders

The Dashboard shows your order total for a given period and other summary information for your site.

Products

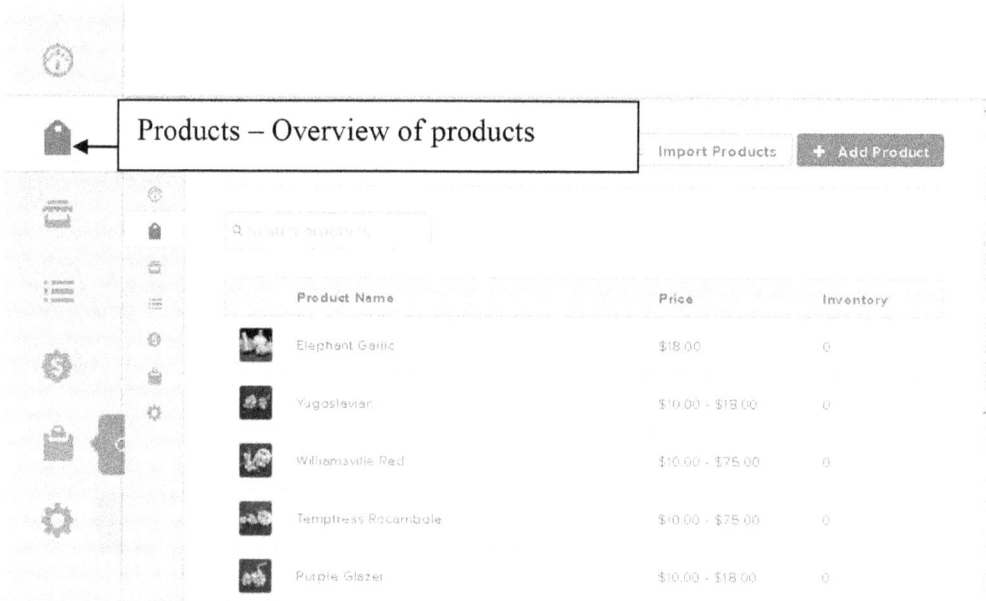

Products – Overview of products

Product Name	Price	Inventory
Elephant Garlic	$18.00	0
Yugoslavian	$10.00 - $18.00	0
Williamsville Red	$10.00 - $75.00	0
Temptress Rocambole	$10.00 - $75.00	0
Purple Glazer	$10.00 - $18.00	0

The Products view is where you manage your products on the store, and where you update inventory. The inventory figures posted here for the $300 version, in the far right hand column, are updated by the Weebly e-commerce when your customer orders. You may update the numbers to reflect non-customer changes in the inventory such as spoilage. After updating the inventory or making any changes to this screen be sure to *Publish* the site, thus storing your changes.

Storefront

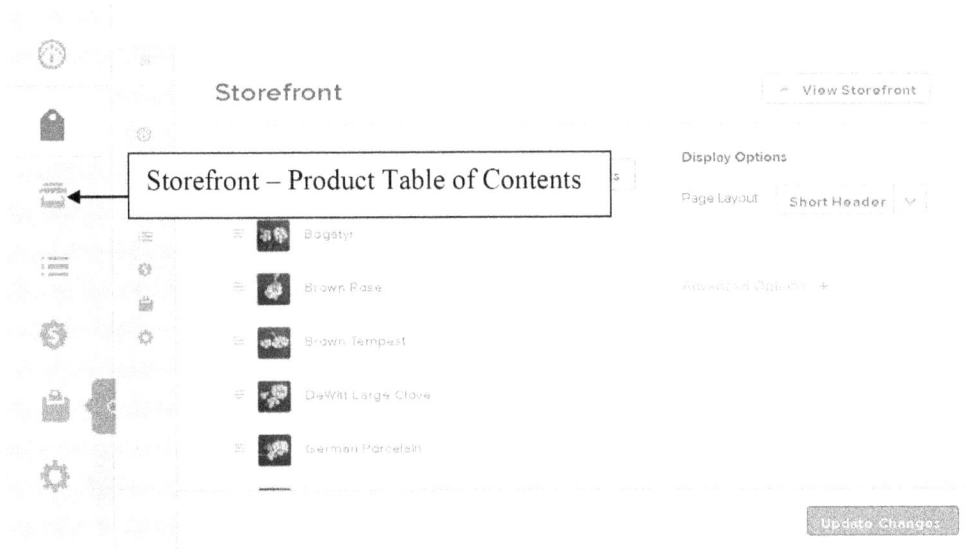

Storefront – Product Table of Contents

For the sake of simplicity we did not use Storefront in our website because it requires setting up categories. Consult Weebly Help Center to learn how to set up categories for your website, and thus qualify your site to implement a *table of contents* storefront.

Categories

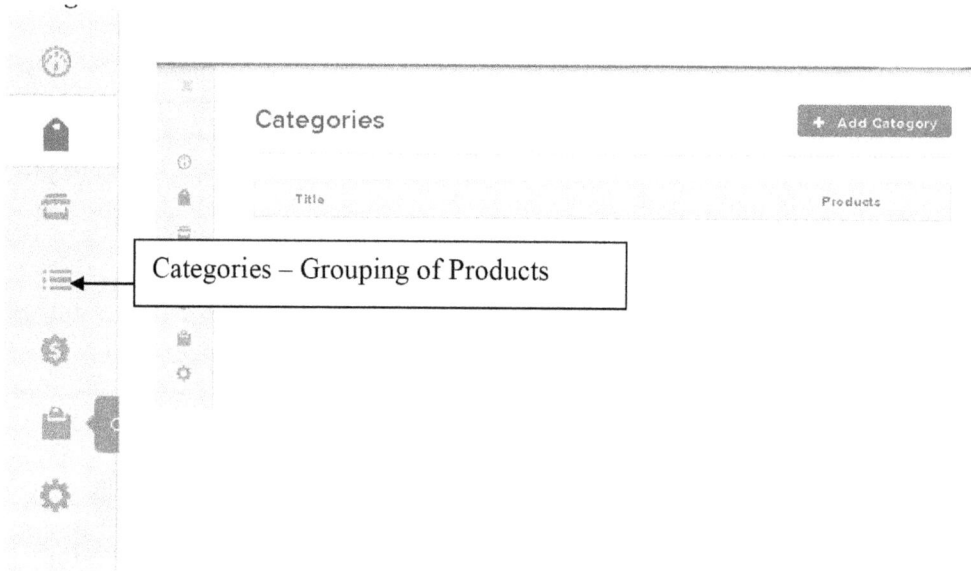

Since we did not use Categories please consult *Weebly Help Center* for setting up categories.

Coupons

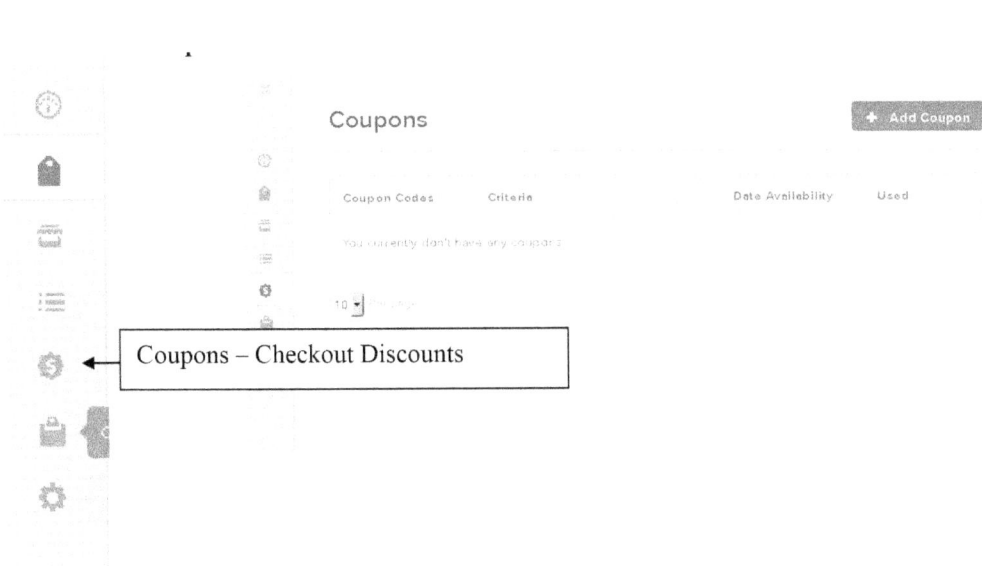

Coupons – Checkout Discounts

Coupons are not used on our site. See Weebly Help Center.

Orders

The list of your orders received is always available to to you to be selected by date. This is the screen where you export orders for off-line processing. This screen shows Order Number, Order Date, Customer Name, Order Status (Pending, Shipped, etc.) and Total Amount. By clicking on the Order Number you can bring up the order detail shown on the following screen.

Order #1726161828

Print Order

Order Details

Item	Price	Qty	Total
Purple Glazer Seed Garlic: One Pound Bag	$18.00	1	$18.00

Subtotal	$18.00
Tax	$0.00
Shipping	$12.35

Order Notes
Margaret, This order shows a one pound bag at $18. You will actually receive two 1/2 pound bags. Best regards, Richard.

Settings – Overall

TOTAL $30.35

↩ Issue Refund

✔ Mark As Returned

Settings

Clicking on Settings in the Administrative Overview menu bring up the following submenu.

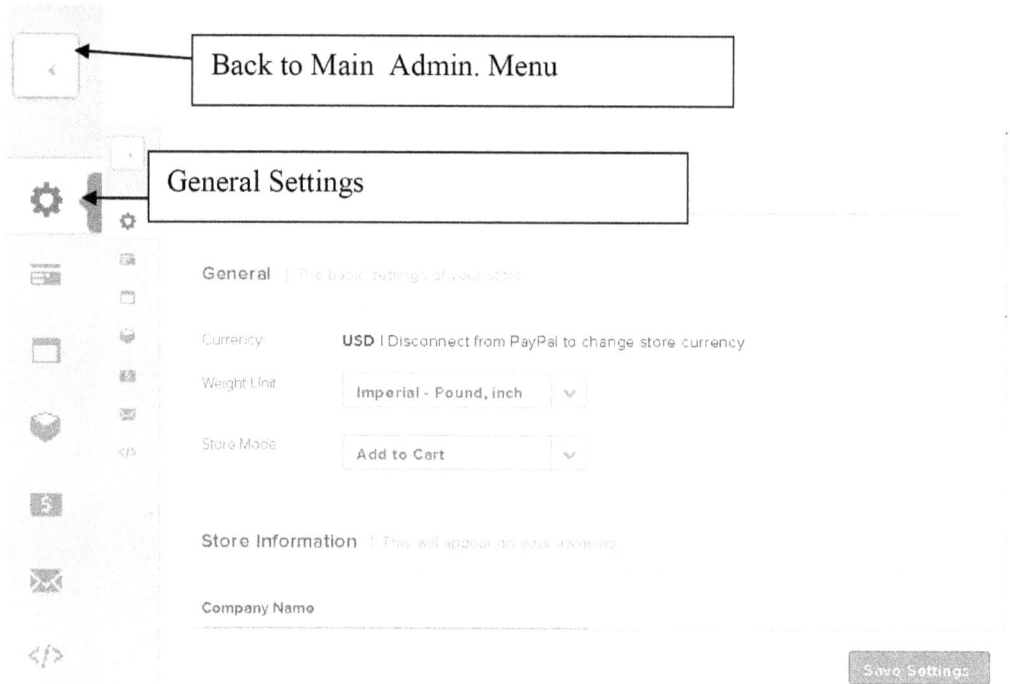

General Settings allows you to establish the currency for the store, the company address, the store policies and an indicator if you would like a text box in the shopping cart which the customer has the option to complete.

Checkout Options

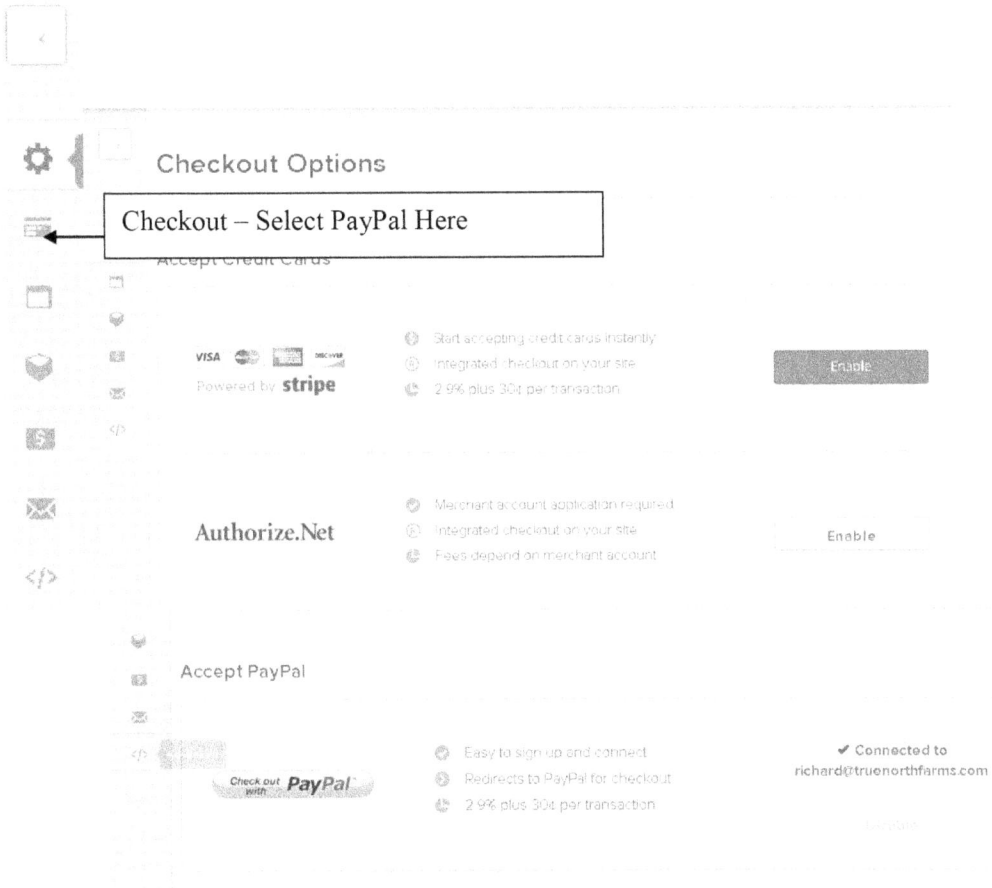

Checkout Options

Checkout – Select PayPal Here

Accept Credit Cards

VISA · · · Powered by **stripe**

- Start accepting credit cards instantly
- Integrated checkout on your site
- 2.9% plus 30¢ per transaction

Enable

Authorize.Net

- Merchant account application required
- Integrated checkout on your site
- Fees depend on merchant account

Enable

Accept PayPal

Check out **PayPal** with

- Easy to sign up and connect
- Redirects to PayPal for checkout
- 2.9% plus 30¢ per transaction

✔ Connected to
richard@truenorthfarms.com

This is where you establish the link between PayPal and Weebly. Your Weebly ID, in this case our email address, creates the link. It is active the minute you set it up. If you are using inventory control, by keeping zero inventories on hand, you will prevent anyone from ordering prematurely. We will tell you how we tested our site at a later point in the narrative. This guide depends on you choosing PayPal. All of the fulfillment, described later, is dependent on PayPal.

Display

Display Options

Store Layout

Columns of products   2 3 4 6

Products per page   24 36 48 60 72

Display

Product Image   3x2   4x3   1x1   3x4   2x3

Save Settings

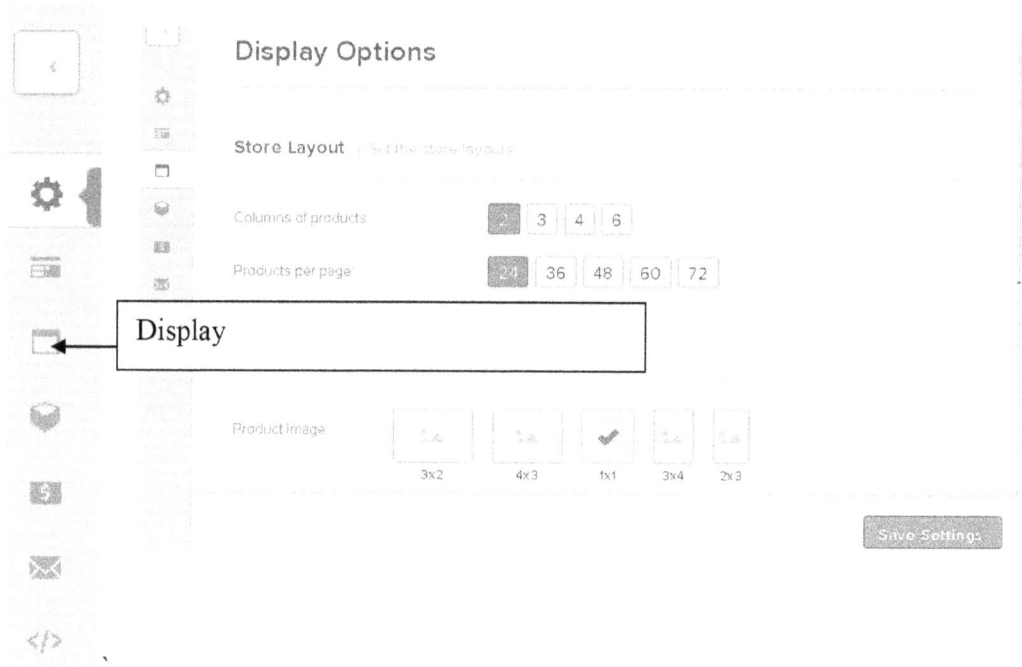

This is the display to format your storefront. Since we didn't use Categories this section simply shows default values. See Weebly Help Center for directions for using this screen.

Shipping

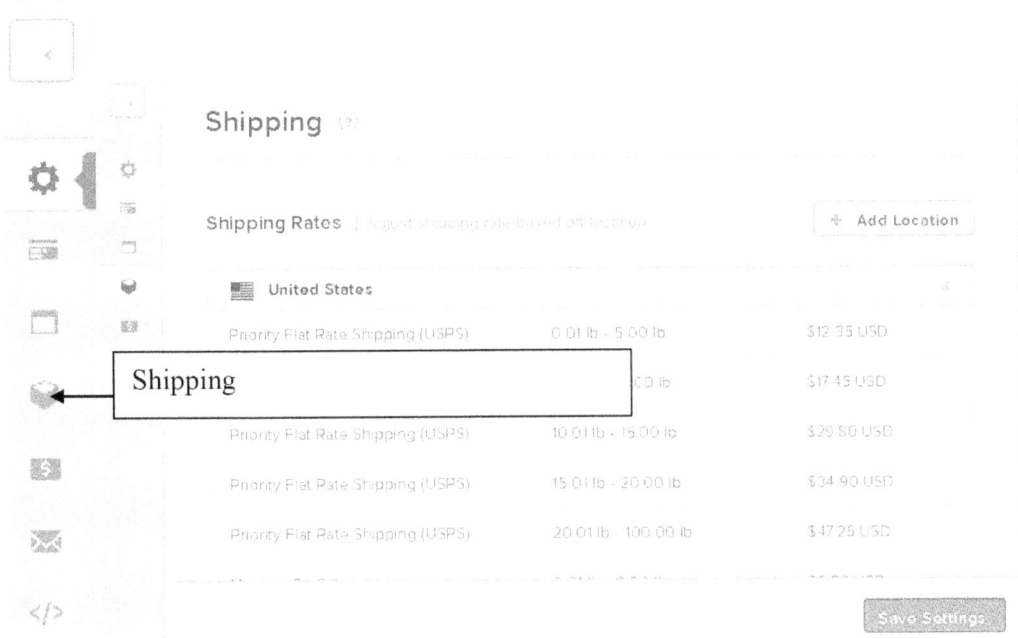

This listing shows all of the shipping options that have been selected. If you click on +Add Rate at the bottom of the screen or on one of the line items, the box below will pop up and you can enter the detailed shipping information. Noted below is the Edit Shipping Rate box for shipping by dollar value; following that, we show an example of shipping by weight. Be sure to click on Edit Sub regions on this option even if you have made no changes, it may be necessary to get your selection stored.

Edit Shipping Rate

Shipping Title

Order $.01 - $10.00

Based On:

| Price | Weight |

Price Range (optional)

0.01 - 10

Shipping Price

4

Edit Subregions   Cancel   Save

Our Standard Shipping Charges by dollar value:

Order Subtotal	Add Shipping Charges
$.01 - $10.00	$4.00
$10.01 - $30.00	$6.75
$30.01 - $50.00	$10.00
$50.01-$100.00	$12..35
$100.01 - $200.00	$17.45
$200.01 +	Free

Edit Shipping Rate

Shipping Title

Priority Flat Rate Shipping (USPS)

Based On:

Price | **Weight**

Weight Range (optional)

0.01 — 5

Shipping Price

12.35

Edit Subregions

Cancel | Save

This screen shows that for Priority USPS Flat Rate Shipping for weights between .01 and 5 pounds the Shipping Price will be $12.35. This is the 2014 rate which, of course will change over time. The creation of estimated shipping charges is one of the more complicated aspects of using Weebly E-Commerce. If the USPS flat rate charges are used as the base it simplifies the creation of a shipping table.

For the remaining rates we started with the postal zone charts that can be accessed at the following web site – http://postcalc.usps.gov/ZoneCharts/Default.aspx

Postal zones are calculated from your current location. For example, we input 049, the first three digits of our *ship from* zip code. The table below lists the destination three digit zip codes associated with their region. The post office charges different rates for each zone 1 to 9.

UNITED STATES POSTAL SERVICE. Postal Zone Charts

Postal

Get Zone Chart | Get Zone for ZIP Code Pair

Get Zone Chart

Enter the first 3-digits of the origin ZIP Code: 049   Get Zone Chart   Print Friendly
(For example, for ZIP Code 12345 use 123)

3-digit ZIP Code prefix is 049. The first 3-digits of your destination ZIP Code determine th
* Indicates ZIP Code range within the same NDC as the origin ZIP Code
+ Indicates ZIP Code range has 5-Digit Exceptions

ZIP Code	Zone	ZIP Code	Zone	ZIP Code	Zone	ZIP Code	Zone
005	4	298	6	537---540	6	719---725	6
006---009	8	299	5	541---543	5	726---727	7
010---038	3*	300---329	6	544	6	728	6
039---043	2*	330---333	7	545	5	729---731	7
044	1*	334---338	6	546---548	6	733	8
045	2*	339---341	7	549	5	734---738	7
046---047	1*	342	6	550---551	6	739	8
048	2*	344	6	553---567	6	740---741	7
049	1*	346---347	6	570---575	6	743---764	7
050---065	3*	349---352	6	576---577	7	765	8
066	4	354---364	6	580---584	6	766---767	7
067	3*	365---366	7	585---588	7	768---769	8
068---098	4	367---368	6	590---599	8	770	7
100---119	4	369	7	600---608	5	772---778	7
120---123	3*	370---375	6	609	6	779---816	8
124---127	4	376---379	5	610---611	5	820---838	8
128---129	3*	380---386	6	612---620	6	840---847	8
130---149	4	387	7	622---631	6	850---853	8

The following map taken from Wiki Commons may be accessed at:

http://upload.wikimedia.org/wikipedia/commons/thumb/2/24/ZIP_Code_zones.svg/2000px-ZIP_Code_zones.svg.png

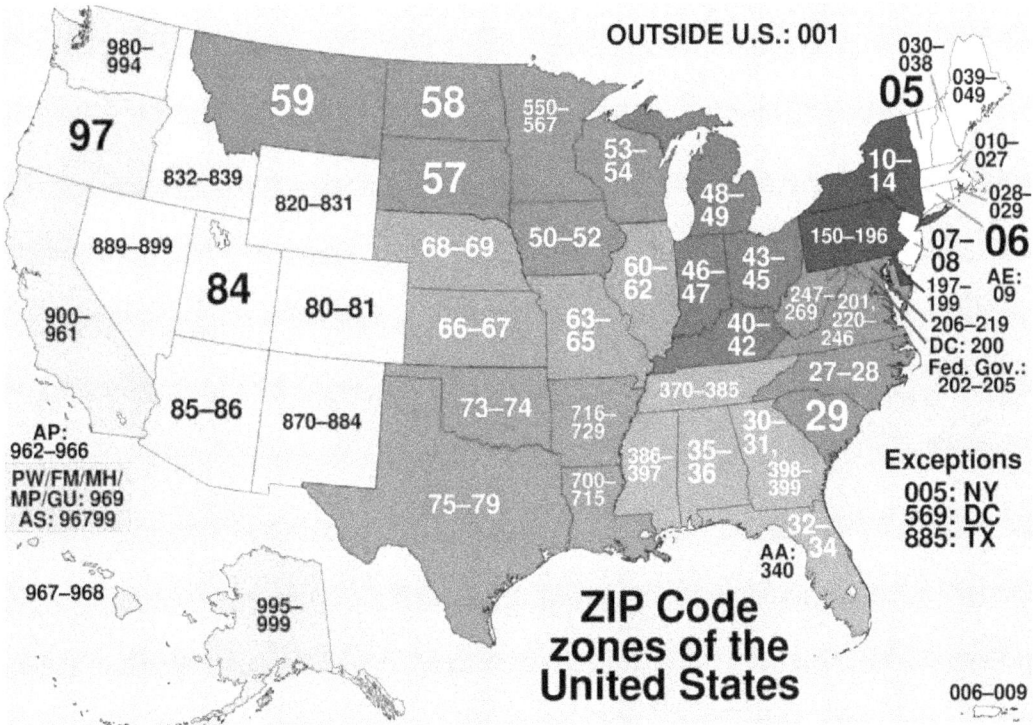

ZIP Code zones of the United States

By combining the Postal Zone chart for your 3 digit zip code with the above map you should be able to create at least a subset of your shipping charge table. We looked at the most common shipping locations close to us and then for longer shipments routinely charged the USPS Priority Mail Flat Rate shipping charge (one, two or max 3 day service). If the rate was too high for a small delivery we refunded the charge via PayPal. You need to be creative with these tables as the chore of creating tables for every possible combination of weight shipping situations is simply too daunting for the average small business. That is why we recommend charging shipping based on the dollar value of the shipment.

Taxes

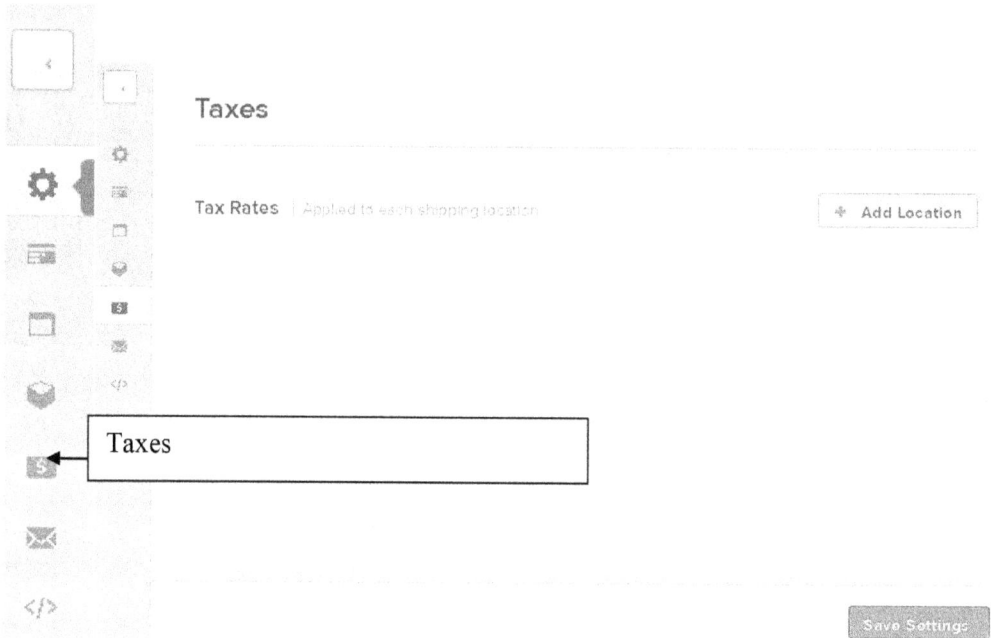

Tax rates for your various locations may be input on the above screen.

Emails

Emails

Reply-to address: **richard@truenorthfarms.com** Edit

Email Type

Order Confirmation

Download Confirmation

Shipped Email

Email Messages   28

Canceled Email

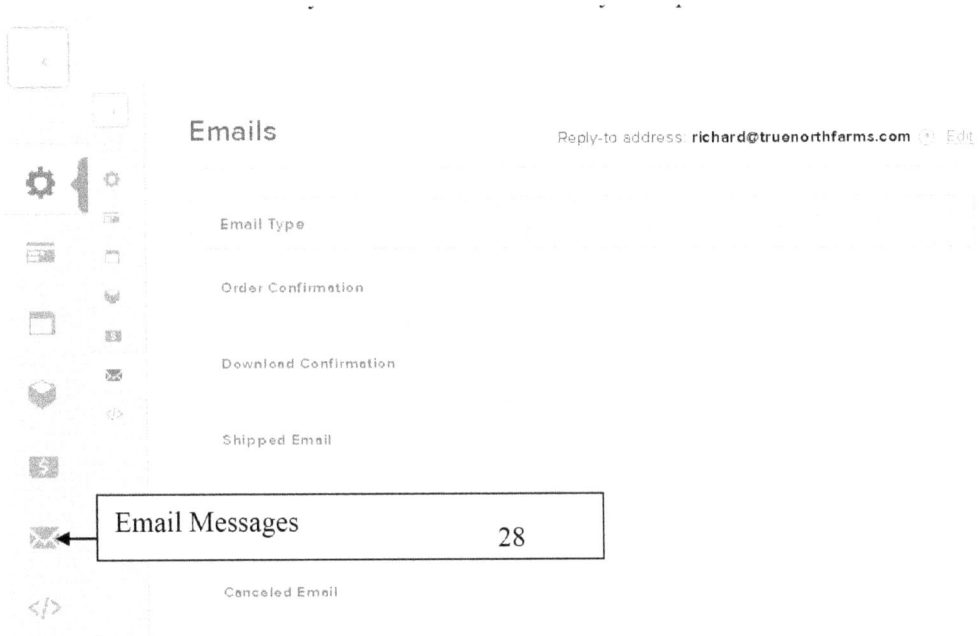

The screen above will show you the list of emails sent for each of the listed transaction types. The other confirmation emails are similar. They may be edited. Noted below is the format of the Order Confirmation.

Order Confirmation

True North Farms, Inc.
(OrganicMaineGarlic.com)

Order
Confirmation
#12345678

Thank you for your order!

Click here to add a header message

Shipping Address

John Doe
123 Anywhere Road
Nowhere, CA 99999
USA

Billing Information

Visa Transaction # 000000
John Doe
123 Anywhere Road
Nowhere, CA 99999

Order Receipt

Widget
Quantity: 2 @ $20.00 each

Gadget
Size: Small

Subtotal $43.99
Shipping - Priority Flat Rate Shipping (USPS)

Advanced Settings

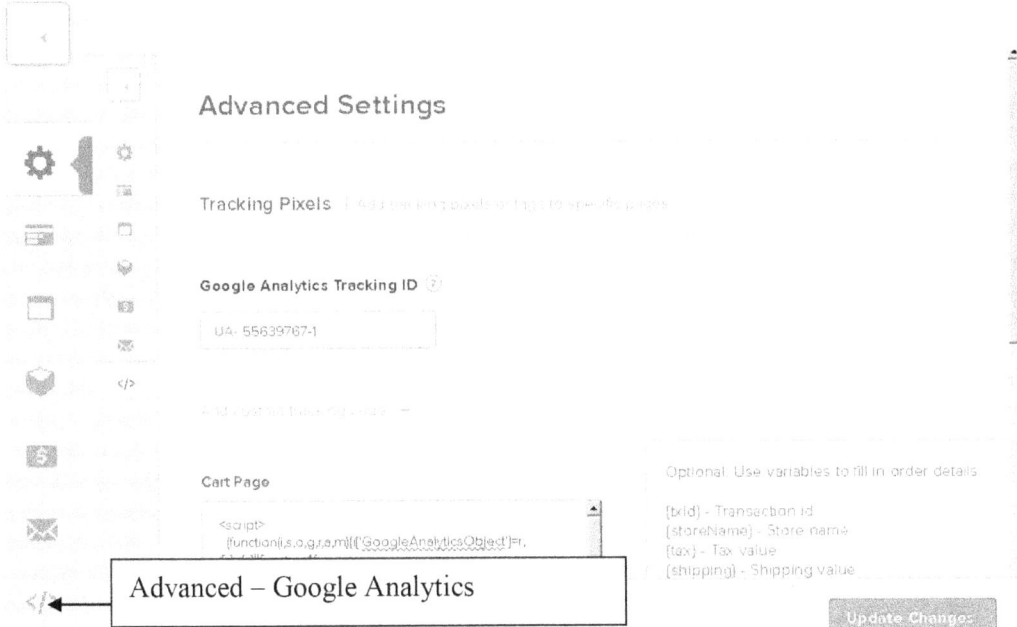

Advanced – Google Analytics

The Advanced screen is used to implement Google Analytics on your site. This is not recommended until you have been working with the site for some time. Google Analytics, a free service that provides statistics on how your site is used. Canned scripts supplied by Google may be inserted into the automatically generated HTML code on your site at the Cart, Payment and Receipt pages. You will be able to track how many sales conversions you have had and thus evaluate the effectiveness of your site. We suggest getting Google help to implement Analytics.

Service Providers

Before continuing our presentation of the Seed Garlic Order Process Flow Chart shown at the beginning of this section I would like to review the various service providers that are prerequisites to a working e-commerce system. The four providers that are necessary are:

1. Domain registrar

    If possible you will want your own domain for Weebly, Google Adwords and PayPal. We register all of our domains with Go Daddy. Weebly can also handle domain registration.

2. Weebly login and email

    Since organicmainegarlic.com is a sub-unit of True North Farms I used richard@truenorthfarms.com as my Weebly login and my email address. Weebly is able to keep track of the fact that www. organicmainegarlic.com is a sub-unit of True North Farms. You will see that in the sample of our Order Confirmation email above. We have no email support for organicmainegarlic.com because, as sub-set of the farm, we are using truenorthfarms.com email.

3. Google Adwords login and email

    richard@truenorthfarms.com is also my Google Adwords login and email.

4. PayPal login and email

    richard@truenorthfarms.com is also my PayPal login and email.

5. Email registration

   In the event that you need a native email for your e-commerce site you will need to register with an email provider. The path of least resistance is to order your domain and email with Weebly. The mere fact that you are using Weebly implies that you will be hosting with Weebly.

We use GoDaddy to register our domains and FatCow for our email. If you choose to do the same, there are instructions on these sites that will show how to proceed. Weebly has instructions for redirecting web traffic from GoDaddy to Weebly. FatCow has instructions how to redirect your email traffic from GoDaddy to FatCow.

We move now to Item #2 in the Seed Garlic Order Process Flow Chart. We will return to the e-commerce flow when we discuss PayPal later in this guide.

Creation of Text Ads (Node 2)

Text ads created off-line

The first step in using Google Adwords is to create text ads. We create the ads off-line in a Word document before entering them to Google Adwords. We will discuss registering for Google Adwords when we advance to Item #3 in the Seed Garlic Order Process Flow Chart. Our Google ads are noted below. Google Adwords asks you to group your ads in a two-level hierarchy, first by *campaign* and second by *ad group*. In the case of our site, www.OrganicMaineGarlic.com, our Campaign #1 could be called 2014 Seed Garlic Sales. Our two *Ad Groups* were focused on two constituents in the target audience, Ad Group #1 Small

Farmers and Ad Group #2 Home Gardeners. Each Ad Group has a set of unique keywords. The italicized keywords were keywords that the Google software initially suggested but were abandoned because they failed to attract sufficient *click-throughs*, defined as a prospective customer clicking their mouse on an ad, the measurement of success. Google Adwords tracks *impressions* the number of times your ad actually appears to someone searching for your product or in the context of a likely cohort of individuals in a non-search medium such as a newsletter. You don't pay for impressions, but you do pay for click throughs. However, if your ad has too low a click through rate, it will not be placed as high or as often by Google's software. Over time Google Adwords presents the statistics for the non-producing keywords so the list of keywords can be pared down to a more productive list. The more productive your ads, usually the more orders you get. The lists below show the productive keywords in normal type and the rejected keywords in italics for each of the Ad Groups that we launched for our seed garlic sales campaign. You will also notice that there are no key-word duplications between Ad Group #1 and Ad Group #2. This is a deliberate strategy as it improves the differentiation between the two groups. I learned all of the above information from using Google Adwords, but more importantly by calling their absolutely stellar Worldwide Phone Support. You will see *Call Out* groups listed in the keyword list below. If your ad ranks in the top three for a particular keyword search, the Call Outs will be listed under your ad in the main body of the search results at the top of the list, and will access a subset of your site directly. It is best to get Google Adwords technical support help in creating Call Outs. What we mention here is the tip of a very sophisticated piece of software that I can appreciate only as a beginning user.

Box ad examples are shown below:

Ad Group #1 –Small Farmer	
Seed Garlic for Sale	**Productive Keywords**
Winter hardy Maine garlic seed	organic garlic
U. Maine tested – MOFGA certified	garlic bulbs
www.organicmainegarlic.com	garlic growing
	garlic seed
Organic Garlic for Sale	garlic seed for sale
Ten varieties still in stock	garlic farming
U. Maine tested – MOFGA certified	heirloom garlic
www.organicmainegarlic.com	hardneck garlic
	German porcelain garlic
Organic Growers' Garlic	porcelain garlic
Ten varieties still in stock	Inchelium Red garlic
U. Maine tested – MOFGA certified	Purple Glazer garlic
www.organicmainegarlic.com	Yugoslavian garlic
Call outs:	**Non-Productive Keywords**
View best practices (19)	*softneck garlic*
Explore our process (19)	*organic grower*
Next day shipping (17)	*organic garlic grower*
Browse by type or variety (25)	*organic seed garlic*
	Transylvanian garlic
Max characters for:	*planting garlic*
Headline – (25) characters	*garlic bulbs for sale*
Ad Line 1 (35) characters	*how to grow garlic*
Ad Line 2 (35) characters	*how to plant garlic*
Ad Line 3 (35) characters	*garlic planting*
	garlic for planting
	garlic bulbs for planting
	bogatyr garlic

Ad Group #2 –Home Gardener	
Free Garlic Planting Guide	**Productive Keywords**
Buy garlic for your home garden	organic garlic seed
U. Maine tested – MOFGA certified	how to plant garlic
www.organicmainegarlic.com	growing garlic at home
	garlic for planting
Grow garlic at home	organic garlic for planting
Organic garlic seed	organic garlic seed for sale
U. Maine tested – MOFGA certified	large clove garlic
www.organicmainegarlic.com	planting organic garlic
	garlic planting guide
Add garlic to your garden	garlic varieties for sale
Organic garlic seed for sale	organic garlic to plant
U. Maine tested – MOFGA certified	
www.organicmainegarlic.com	**Non-Productive Keywords**
	cultivate garlic at home
	growing garlic in the home garden
	planting garlic seeds in the home garden
	seed garlic for home
	organic garlic seed for sale
	bulk organic garlic
	garlic rocambole
	porcelain garlic varieties

Launching Google AdWords (Node 3)

Register with Google

The first step in using Google Adwords is to register with Google. The registration process will ask you to register a unique email address, create a tough password, register a credit card, and establish a daily budget and so forth. For organicmainegarlic.com I established a budget of $5.00 a day. Over five weeks I spent less than $150 with the $5 a day budget figure to get 4,000 visits to my website and enough conversions to sell out my seed garlic crop. It struck me as a really good deal. This budget will need to be increased to $10 a day in 2015 in order to qualify for free support.

Establish Keywords

The second step is to establish your keywords and write your ads as mentioned above. I was coached by Google to tie my keywords into both the box ads and the website. It is a good idea to cross-reference both to ensure that the Google software will do the best job displaying your ads.

Activate Google

Once your website is ready to handle traffic you can activate Google. When you turn it on you will starting getting traffic right away. They look for about a 1% click through rate. If you are getting less they will coach you with suggested improvements so you will get that rate.

No Redirection

Here are a couple of cautions: first, your website cannot be a redirect, it must be a native landing spot URL; second, your ads must be approved by Google before they are listed. It takes a bit of time before your ads begin to show. My ads usually showed in a couple of hours.

Let it run

After your website is approved and all your ads are running let the system run for a while and see how you are doing. The Google Adwords Campaign Management gives you many metrics to see how your ads are playing. After your campaign has been running for a few days call the Google help line to get advice on how to improve. They will help you get better results. I followed their advice to the letter and found that my volume of click throughs increased as well as my sales conversion rates. Over the course of my first campaign, I logged a couple of hours with the technicians in several separate calls. Each call yielded great advice that worked when I applied it.

Google AdWords screenshots

I include a few screen shots of our organicmainegarlic Google Adwords Campaign Management screens so you begin to get the flavor of the system. I can't begin to tutor you in how to use it. My only advice is, plunge in, and don't be afraid to call Google. They are tremendously helpful, and they don't charge for the calls if you have a budget of $10 a day or more.

A Google AdWords   Home   Campaigns   Opportunities   Tools

Customer ID: 381-518-9365 ▾   ⚙   🔔
richard@truenorthfarms.com

⚠ **None of your ads are running (Last updated: 5 hours ago)** · Your campaigns and ad groups are paused or removed. Enable them to begin showing your ads.
Guide me | Learn more

Customize modules   All time: Jan 1, 2001 - Feb 5, 2015 ▾

📁 All campaigns ▾   ▤ Clicks ▾   vs   None ▾   Monthly ▾

Clicks	Impr.	CTR	Avg. CPC	Cost
373	**39,504**	**0.94%**	**$0.31**	**$115.49**

⌘ **Top movers latest 7-day report**   –   ⌶ Performance graph

No Top Movers reports are available

✎ Good quality but low traffic keywords (54)   ▾ – ✕

Keyword	‹ Clicks	Cost	CTR	Impr.	Avg. CPC ›
⊚ garlic seed for sale	19	$5.36	4.62%	411	$0.28
⊚ hardneck garlic	7	$1.71	0.99%	707	$0.24
⊚ growing garlic at home	6	$0.93	10.71%	56	$0.16
⊚ garlic farming	5	$1.35	0.89%	559	$0.27
⊚ heirloom garlic	5	$1.71	1.49%	336	$0.34

View saved filter ›   1-5 of 54   ‹   ›

✎ All enabled keywords (0)   ▾ – ✕

No matching keywords.

📁 All enabled campaigns (0)   ▾ – ✕

No matching campaigns.

All enabled ad groups (0)   ▾ – ✕

No matching ad groups.

✎ Keywords below first page bid (0)   ▾ – ✕

No matching keywords.

✎ All non-active keywords (80)   ▾ – ✕

Keyword	‹ Clicks	Cost	CTR	Impr.	Avg. CPC ›
⊚ garlic seed	60	$15.30	1.56%	3,857	$0.26
⊚ how to plant garlic	40	$9.94	3.11%	1,288	$0.25
⊚ garlic bulbs	34	$10.42	0.93%	3,671	$0.31
⊚ organic garlic	21	$6.17	1.19%	1,772	$0.29
⊚ garlic seed for sale	19	$5.36	4.62%	411	$0.28

View saved filter ›   1-5 of 80   ‹   ›

📁 All non-active campaigns (2)   ▾ – ✕

Campaign	‹ Status	Clicks	Cost	Impr.	CTR ›
⫙ Campaign #1	Paused	369	$113.45	39,407	0.94%
⫙ Campaign #2	Paused	4	$2.04	97	4.12%

View saved filter ›

Google and the Google logo are registered trademarks of Google, Inc., used with permission.

4

....

Fulfillment from Weebly and PayPal (Nodes 4-8)

Fulfillment of orders is the last step in this e-commerce solution. The fulfill-ment support is available from standard PayPal reports.

Weebly Download

Weebly supports a CSV download which provides all the detail of the order including the detail transactions and the amount of shipping charged to the customer. The format of the CSV file is documented in Appendix 1.0. This download file will be helpful when you attempt to enter your sales data to your accounting system.

PayPal Packing Slip (Node 5)

PayPal has an impressive array of fulfillment supports. Under the best circumstances you should have created a separate domain name for your e-commerce effort. If this is not feasible, you should create separate email accounts for your e-commerce logins including PayPal. The benefit of a private domain pointing to FatCow is you can set up several email accounts at no additional charge for each account. An alternative to this would be to set up new Gmail accounts for your e-commerce emails. In these examples, however, we will focus on the dedicated domain as the approach. After you log into PayPal you will navigate from the PayPal dashboard noted below and the Detail List that follows.

Activity	Bookkeeping	Charts & Graphs
0	$0.00	$0.00
payments received in the last 30 days	received in February 2015	received in current quarter

Activity

Email Address ▾ Search

| Custom | Monthly | Quarterly | Yearly | 9/21/2014 | To | 2/9/2015 | View |

I'm looking for All transactions ▾ In All currencies ▾ From September 21, 2014 to February 9, 2015 Download

☐ Include archived transactions

| Dec 6, 2014 | Transfer To Bank Account Completed | Archive ▾ | -$94.75 USD |
| Nov 8, 2014 | Fee reversal From PayPal Completed | Archive ▾ | $4.06 USD |

Oct 11, 2014	PayPal services To US Postal Service Completed Shipped	Track ▼	-$7.25 USD
Oct 11, 2014	PayPal services To US Postal Service Completed Shipped	Track ▼	-$11.58 USD
Oct 11, 2014	PayPal services To US Postal Service Completed Shipped	Track ▼	-$7.55 USD
Oct 10, 2014	Payment From Alice Rodgers Completed Shipped	Track ▼	$44.15 USD
Oct 10, 2014	Payment From G_____e Completed Shipped	Track ▼	$146.20 USD
Oct 10, 2014	PayPal services To US Postal Service Completed Shipped	Track ▼	-$15.80 USD
Oct 10, 2014	PayPal services To US Postal Service Completed Shipped	Track ▼	-$7.55 USD

When you click on one of the transactions in the detail above you will display the detail transaction as noted below.

P PayPal ⌂   Money   Transactions   Customers   Tools   More ▾   Log Out

Transaction Details

✓ **Shipped** Track   Payment Status: Completed

What should I do now?

- Ship to the buyer's address on this page.
- Ship using a shipping service that provides signature confirmation.
- Save all tracking information or other proof of shipment.

Tips to sell securely

Seller Protection

Eligible (More about Seller Protection)

Seller Protection address

Confirmed ■▪

Shopping Cart Payment Received (Unique Transaction ID #7JB565555U000382X)

Name: _____ nder of this payment is **Unregistered**)
Email:
Payment Sent to: richard@truenorthfarms.com

59

Shopping Cart Contents

Qty	Item	Options	Price
1	German Porcelain	Seed Garlic: Half Pound Bag	$10.00 USD
1	Temptress Rocambole	Seed Garlic: Half Pound Bag	$10.00 USD
1	Purple Glazer	Seed Garlic: One Pound Bag	$18.00 USD
		Amount	$38.00 USD

Order Description: Shopping Cart
Item Total: $38.00 USD
Sales Tax: $0.00 USD
Shipping: $6.15 USD
Handling: $0.00 USD

Total amount: $44.15 USD
Fee amount: -$1.58 USD
Net amount: $42.57 USD

Date: Oct 10, 2014
Time: 15:47:20 PDT
Status: Completed

Payment Type: Instant

Shipment Information

Shipping Status: Shipped
Reference Number: U.S. Postal Service 9405909699939304747664 Learn More

Total Shipping Cost: $7.25 USD

The above PayPal transaction detail record shows you the complete information on your customer. The bottom of this screen is shown on the next page.

It is from this screen you can produce the Packing Slip as well as the prepaid postage/shipping label.

Payment Type: Instant

Shipment Information

Shipping Status: Shipped
Reference Number: U.S. Postal Service 9405909699939304747664 Learn More

Total Shipping Cost: $7.25 USD

Shipping:
[Print Packing Slip | Ship Another] 🔲

See transaction 9D912678LK082084W for further details about your shipping label.

Description: Shopping Cart
Refund:
To refund this payment in part or full for any reason, please use the Send Money tab. The Refund Payment option is available for 60 days after a payment was sent.

Return to Log

The Packing Slip set-up is displayed below.

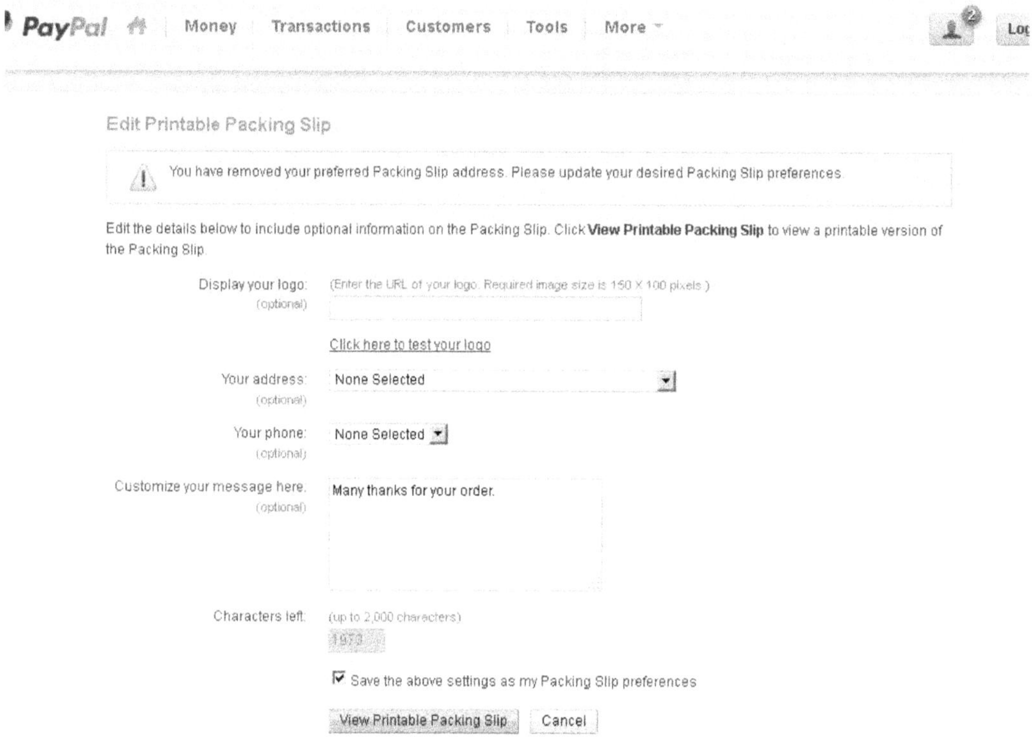

The Packing Slip output is displayed on the next page.

PayPal

Packing Slip

Ship To:

Address:

Email:

Ship From: True North Farms, Inc.
http://organicmainegarlic.com

Email: richard@truenorthfarms.com

Transaction ID: 7JB565555U000382X

Description	Options	Qty	Price
German Porcelain	Seed Garlic: Half Pound Bag	1	$10.00 USD
Temptress Rocambole	Seed Garlic: Half Pound Bag	1	$10.00 USD
Purple Glazer	Seed Garlic: One Pound Bag	1	$18.00 USD

Shipping & Handling: $6.15 USD
Sales Tax: $0.00 USD
Total: $44.15 USD
This is not a bill.

Note: Many thanks for your order.

Print | Edit | Done

Our fulfillment procedure is detailed below. You can adapt it to your circumstances.

PayPal Prepaid Shipping Label (Node 6)

Custom: [   ], This order shows a one pound bag at $18. You will actually receive two 1/2 pound bags. Best regards, Richard.

Date: Oct 11, 2014

Time: 14:27:00 PDT

Status: Completed

Payment Type: Instant

Shipment Information

Shipping Status: Shipped

Reference Number: U.S. Postal Service 9405509699938827745968 Learn More

Total Shipping Cost: $5.44 USD

Shipping:
[Print Packing Slip | Ship Another]

See transaction 56X81743R2888121D for further details about your shipping label.

Description: Shopping Cart

Refund:
To refund this payment in part or full for any reason, please use the Send Money tab. The Refund Payment option is available for 60 days after a payment was sent.

Return to Log

The following screen permits you to request a preprinted shipping label. You will note that this screen says, *Ship another?* The first time one prints it says *Print Shipping Label?* The *Ship another* feature means you can weigh and print a label for each package in a multi-package delivery. In addition to printing the multiple labels I always mark on the boxes, for example, if there are two, 1 of 2, and 2 of 2. I also indicate that multiple boxes are being shipped so that the customer will be looking for more than one, more than one box in case the boxes get separated and arrive on different days. Print set-up is shown first and then a sample of a prepaid label second.

U.S. Postal Service - Create Your Shipping Label

Create, purchase, and print U.S. Postal Service® shipping labels from your PayPal account. Complete the form below to prepare y shipping label, or to print multiple shipping labels, go to PayPal MultiOrder shipping. For more information, visit the PayPal shippin or view our brief demo.

Address Information

Ship from	True North Farms, Inc.	Ship to	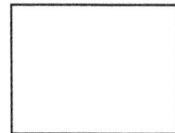
	900 WOODMANS MILL ROAD		
	MONTVILLE ME		
	04941		
	United States		
	Edit address		Edit address

Origination ZIP Code™ ⦿ Same as return address   Status Confirmed address
                ○ Other

Shipment Information

Carrier   U.S. Postal Service Choose a different carrier

Service type   Select Service ▾

Package size   Select One ▾ Learn More About Package Sizes

Weight   lbs.   oz.   More info

Shipment Options

Mailing date   2/10/2015 ▾ More info

Display postage value on label   ○ Yes ⦿ No

Email message to recipient
(optional)

You will notice in the upper left corner the weight of the package, the Postal Zone of the recipient is automatically calculated by PayPal. PayPal also calculates the shipping amount and debits your account automatically when you okay the printing of the label.

4

....

Fulfillment from Weebly and PayPal (Nodes 4-8)

Fulfillment of orders is the last step in this e-commerce solution. The fulfillment support is available from standard PayPal reports.

Weebly Download

Weebly supports a CSV download which provides all the detail of the order including the detail transactions and the amount of shipping charged to the customer. The format of the CSV file is documented in Appendix 1.0. This download file will be helpful when you attempt to enter your sales data to your accounting system.

PayPal Packing Slip (Node 5)

PayPal has an impressive array of fulfillment supports. Under the best circumstances you should have created a separate domain name for your e-commerce effort. If this is not feasible, you should create separate email accounts for your e-commerce logins including PayPal. The benefit of a private domain pointing to FatCow is you can set up several email accounts at no additional charge for each account. An alternative to this would be to set up new Gmail accounts for your e-commerce emails. In these examples, however, we will focus on the dedicated domain as the approach. After you log into PayPal you will navigate from the PayPal dashboard noted below and the Detail List that follows.

Oct 11, 2014	PayPal services To US Postal Service Completed Shipped	Track ▼	-$7.25 USD
Oct 11, 2014	PayPal services To US Postal Service Completed Shipped	Track ▼	-$11.58 USD
Oct 11, 2014	PayPal services To US Postal Service Completed Shipped	Track ▼	-$7.55 USD
Oct 10, 2014	Payment From Alice Rodgers Completed Shipped	Track ▼	$44.15 USD
Oct 10, 2014	Payment From G▭▭▭e Completed Shipped	Track ▼	$146.20 USD
Oct 10, 2014	PayPal services To US Postal Service Completed Shipped	Track ▼	-$15.80 USD
Oct 10, 2014	PayPal services To US Postal Service Completed Shipped	Track ▼	-$7.55 USD

When you click on one of the transactions in the detail above you will display the detail transaction as noted below.

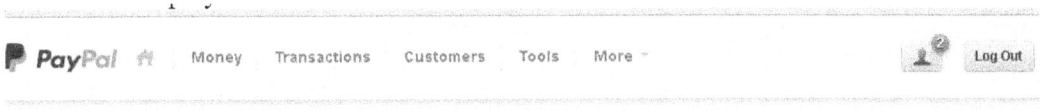

P PayPal ⌂   Money   Transactions   Customers   Tools   More ▾   Log Out

Transaction Details

☑ **Shipped** Track   Payment Status: Completed

What should I do now?   **Seller Protection**

                                                       Eligible (More about Seller Protection)
• Ship to the buyer's address on this page.
• Ship using a shipping service that provides signature   **Seller Protection address**
  confirmation.
• Save all tracking information or other proof of shipment.

Tips to sell securely   Confirmed ▓▓

Shopping Cart Payment Received (Unique Transaction ID #7JB565555U000382X)

                    Name: ▭   nder of this payment is **Unregistered**)
                    Email: ▭
         Payment Sent to: richard@truenorthfarms.com

Shopping Cart Contents

Qty	Item	Options	Price
1	German Porcelain	Seed Garlic: Half Pound Bag	$10.00 USD
1	Temptress Rocambole	Seed Garlic: Half Pound Bag	$10.00 USD
1	Purple Glazer	Seed Garlic: One Pound Bag	$18.00 USD
		Amount	$38.00 USD

Order Description: Shopping Cart
Item Total: $38.00 USD
Sales Tax: $0.00 USD
Shipping: $6.15 USD
Handling: $0.00 USD

Total amount: $44.15 USD
Fee amount: -$1.58 USD
Net amount: $42.57 USD

Date: Oct 10, 2014
Time: 15:47:20 PDT
Status: Completed

Payment Type: Instant

Shipment Information

Shipping Status: Shipped
Reference Number: U.S. Postal Service 9405909699939304747664 Learn More

Total Shipping Cost: $7.25 USD

The above PayPal transaction detail record shows you the complete information on your customer. The bottom of this screen is shown on the next page.

It is from this screen you can produce the Packing Slip as well as the prepaid postage/shipping label.

Payment Type: Instant

Shipment Information

Shipping Status: Shipped
Reference Number: U.S. Postal Service 9405909699939304747664 Learn More

Total Shipping Cost: $7.25 USD

Shipping:
[Print Packing Slip | Ship Another]

See transaction 9D912678LK082084W for further details about your shipping label.

Description: Shopping Cart
Refund:
To refund this payment in part or full for any reason, please use the Send Money tab. The Refund Payment option is available for 60 days after a payment was sent.

Return to Log

The Packing Slip set-up is displayed below.

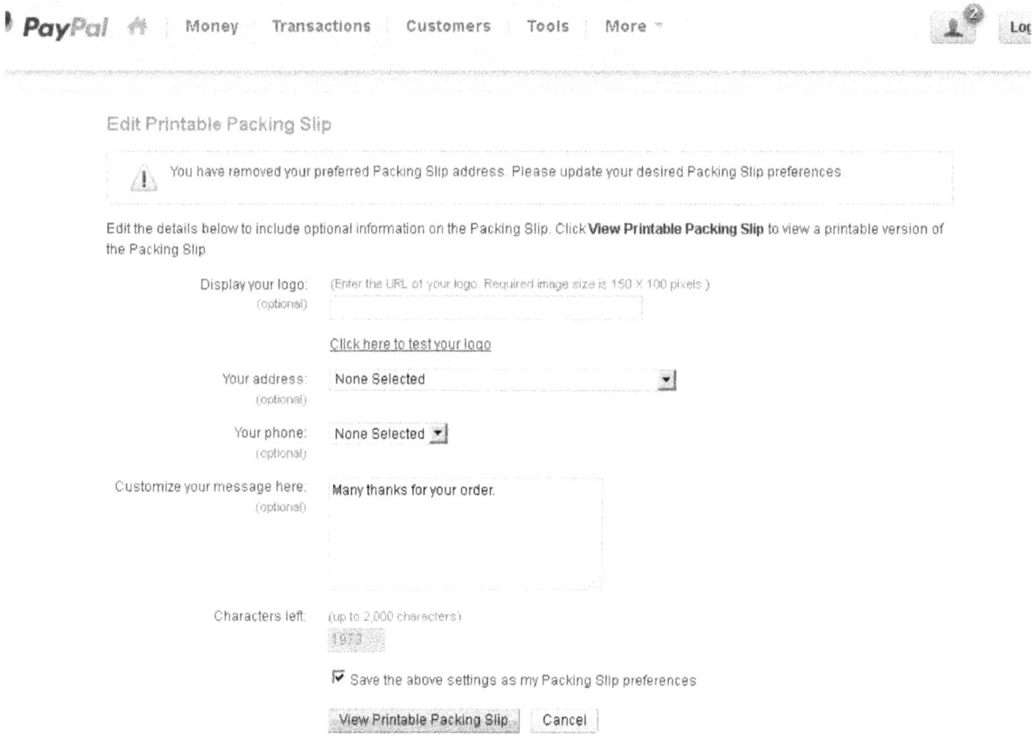

The Packing Slip output is displayed on the next page.

P PayPal

Packing Slip

Ship To:		**Ship From:** True North Farms, Inc.
		http://organicmainegarlic.com
Address:		
Email:		**Email:** richard@truenorthfarms.com

Transaction ID: 7JB565555U000382X

Description	Options	Qty	Price
German Porcelain	Seed Garlic: Half Pound Bag	1	$10.00 USD
Temptress Rocambole	Seed Garlic: Half Pound Bag	1	$10.00 USD
Purple Glazer	Seed Garlic: One Pound Bag	1	$18.00 USD

Shipping & Handling: $6.15 USD

Sales Tax: $0.00 USD

Total: $44.15 USD

This is not a bill.

Note: Many thanks for your order.

| Print | Edit | Done |

Our fulfillment procedure is detailed below. You can adapt it to your circumstances.

PayPal Prepaid Shipping Label (Node 6)

Custom: [   ], This order shows a one pound bag at $18. You will actually receive two 1/2 pound bags. Best regards, Richard.

Date: Oct 11, 2014

Time: 14:27:00 PDT

Status: Completed

Payment Type: Instant

Shipment Information

Shipping Status: Shipped

Reference Number: U.S. Postal Service 9405509699938827745968 Learn More

Total Shipping Cost: $5.44 USD

Shipping:
[Print Packing Slip | Ship Another] ?

See transaction 56X81743R2888121D for further details about your shipping label.

Description: Shopping Cart

Refund:
To refund this payment in part or full for any reason, please use the Send Money tab. The Refund Payment option is available for 60 days after a payment was sent.

Return to Log

The following screen permits you to request a preprinted shipping label. You will note that this screen says, *Ship another?* The first time one prints it says *Print Shipping Label?* The *Ship another* feature means you can weigh and print a label for each package in a multi-package delivery. In addition to printing the multiple labels I always mark on the boxes, for example, if there are two, 1 of 2, and 2 of 2. I also indicate that multiple boxes are being shipped so that the customer will be looking for more than one, more than one box in case the boxes get separated and arrive on different days. Print set-up is shown first and then a sample of a prepaid label second.

U.S. Postal Service - Create Your Shipping Label

Create, purchase, and print U.S. Postal Service® shipping labels from your PayPal account. Complete the form below to prepare y shipping label, or to print multiple shipping labels, go to PayPal MultiOrder shipping. For more information, visit the PayPal shippin or view our brief demo.

Address Information

Ship from	True North Farms, Inc. 900 WOODMANS MILL ROAD MONTVILLE ME 04941 United States Edit address	Ship to

Origination ZIP Code™ ⦿ Same as return address   Status Confirmed address
                      ◯ Other

Edit address

Shipment Information

Carrier   U.S. Postal Service Choose a different carrier

Service type   Select Service ▾

Package size   Select One ▾ Learn More About Package Sizes

Weight   _____ lbs. ___ oz. More info

Shipment Options

Mailing date   2/10/2015 ▾ More info

Display postage value on label   ◯ Yes ⦿ No

Email message to recipient
(optional)

UNITED STATES POSTAL SERVICE

a preferred shipping service on **ebay**

US POSTAGE PAID
Pitney Bowes

02/10/2015
From 04941
1 lbs 0 ozs
Zone 3

PRIORITY MAIL 2-DAY™

e North Farms, Inc.
WOODMANS MILL ROAD
NTVILLE ME 04941

0025

C091

USPS TRACKING #

9405 5099 73

The safer, easier way to pay **PayPal**

You will notice in the upper left corner the weight of the package, the Postal Zone of the recipient is automatically calculated by PayPal. PayPal also calculates the shipping amount and debits your account automatically when you okay the printing of the label.

Warehouse Pick/Pack (Node 7)

Our "warehouse" is the drying barn for our stock shown in the picture below.

Each of our varieties has a sign posted to the front of the drying table to identify the bulbs. All bags and bins are labeled with preprinted labels. We pull the orders directly from the tables pictured. We check the inventory frequently in the Weebly system to make sure that the physical matches the on-line system.

Our order fulfillment procedure is noted below. Even though we are using the cost of the order to calculate the shipping payment, the cost for the actual shipment charged to your business is based on the weight and dimensions of your package box size taking into account shipping distance.

1. 4 lbs. or under

   New England – 7x7x7 box

   Outside New England – Medium Flat Rate USPS Priority Box

2. 5 lbs.

   New England – Medium Uline box

   Outside New England – Medium Flat Rate USPS Box

3. 6 to 10 lbs..

   New England – Large Uline box

   Outside New England – Large Flat Rate USPS Box

4. 11 lbs. up – use multiple boxes in the above sizes

Our Order Fulfillment Checklist

1. New Order email received – print out

2. Log into PayPal and *Print Packing Slip* noted below.

Custom: ~~margaret~~, This order shows a one pound bag at $18. You will actually receive two 1/2 pound bags. Best regards, Richard.
Date: Oct 11, 2014
Time: 14:27:00 PDT
Status: Completed

Payment Type: Instant

Shipment Information

Shipping Status: Shipped
Reference Number: U.S. Postal Service 9405509699938827745968 Learn More

Total Shipping Cost: $5.44 USD

→ **PayPal**

Packing Slip

Ship To: | **Ship From:** True North Farms, Inc.
Address: | http://organicmainegarlic.com
Email: | **Email:** richard@truenorthfarms.com

Transaction ID: 7JB565555U000382X

Description	Options	Qty	Price
German Porcelain	Seed Garlic: Half Pound Bag	1	$10.00 USD
Temptress Rocambole	Seed Garlic: Half Pound Bag	1	$10.00 USD
Purple Glazer	Seed Garlic: One Pound Bag	1	$18.00 USD

Shipping & Handling: $6.15 USD
Sales Tax: $0.00 USD
Total: $44.15 USD
This is not a bill.

Note: Many thanks for your order.

Print | Edit | Done

---

3. Make up box(es) on the second floor of the lower barn.

4. Place Packing Slip in corresponding box.

5. Take boxes and Packing Slip upper barn in a black bin.

6. Place a single piece of newsprint paper in the bottom of each box. Fold a second piece of newsprint for closing the order at the top and place folded newsprint in the sides of the box.

7. Select appropriate bag for each order item. If necessary bag the order and label the bag with the appropriate variety label.

8. Check off each item on the Packing Slip as they are placed in the box.

9. When the picked order is complete, place the Packing Slip back in the box.

10. Weigh the entire order and place the weight on the top right hand corner of the Packing Slip. Fractional pounds must be multiplied by 16 and rounded up by ½ ounce to the next full ounce. Example: 3.15 pounds on the scale – write the 3 on the Packing Slip. .15 pounds x 16 = 2.4 oz. Round to 3 oz. Write the 3 on the Packing Slip. The result is 3 lbs. 3 oz.

11. Take the order boxes back to the Lower Barn in the black bin to the computer.

12. Log into PayPal and access the Transactions tab. On each order click on Shipping Label.

13. Print the Shipping Label. Cut off and trim the label. Staple the USPS Tracking information to the New Order filled form, and place a sequence number in the upper right hand corner. For larger orders we would print the UPS shipping label.

14. Access our Weebly website and hit Edit.

15. From the opening tab hit Store and click on Shipping on the icon menu to the left.

16. Click on each open order. Click on Shipped. This will pop a box where the Tracking Number should be keyed. Leave the Email box checked so the customer will receive the tracking number via email.

17. The order cycle is now complete. Take boxes to the post office and mail. Or in the case of UPS call to schedule a pick-up.

We found that the USPS was the easiest for us to manage. Also, with small volume, for UPS it costs $6 for each day that there is a pick-up. For larger volume orders use UPS.

5

. . . .

Interface with QuickBooks

The interface with QuickBooks is the weakest part of this otherwise powerful troika of systems. We found that the automated interfaces just didn't work. We ended up summarizing our orders in an off-line spreadsheet and posting the summary charges to QuickBooks manually. The various transactions that are needed are as follows:

- Revenue for products

- Revenue for shipping and handling

- Expense for PayPal fee

- Expense for shipping

- Expense for product returns

- Expense for order adjustments such as shipping reductions

6

Testing Your System

Unfortunately neither Weebly nor PayPal provide a testing platform. Once created, as we have described in this publication, the system is live. I was not willing to plunge ahead, promoting our system to the public, without some sort of a test. I will describe how we tested. You may be able to take our methods and design your own testing methodology after reading this.

- Since our ordering methodology was based on Weebly inventory control we were able to block all ordering by setting inventory values to zero.

- We decided to test the system with our own credit cards. All credit card charges put through PayPal can be reversed so the transactions would show up on our credit card but would zero balance after reversal.

- We decided on three items that we would test order. We changed the end of the item name to read xxx Item Name xxx Do Not Order. Just in case someone tried to order during our test.

- We did a test order, first setting the inventory amount on two items to "1" and one other item to "2". We executed the order which took those items out of inventory.

- We printed a packing slip from PayPal.

- We printed a USPS label for the item, putting in an estimated weight, because we were not shipping actual product. After generating the label it is possible to cancel the label and the charge will be reversed in 10 days.

- Shipping charges are difficult to test. If you use the six levels of charges or some variation on it you will be able to test rather easily. With the weight method it will be possible to test only a small fraction of the charge types. In general your testing will be done only to assure yourself that the system you have integrated is working to your expectation. The bulk of your assurances regarding the accuracy of the results are in the hands of Weebly, Google and PayPal.

- We went through an actual order with a friendly customer who gave us feedback on the website ease of use as well as the ordering process. I found this walk-through with an actual user very helpful; if for no other reason than to have assurance that our e-commerce system was working as planned.

7

. . . .

Budget

A sample budget has been prepared to help you plan your approach to using all the elements of Seed Garlic Order Process. The sample budget is attached below. This example shows a hypothetical product with a price of $80.00 (the average value of our 2014 seed garlic orders) and shows how the Google Adwords, Weebly, PayPal Fees and hypothetical shipping costs vary based on certain volume assumptions. The main purpose of this exhibit is to show you the relationship between *click through* rates and cost per click coupled with *daily budget* to illustrate costs that you might be facing when using the three pieces of software discussed in Seed Garlic Order Process. The Seed Garlic Order Process spreadsheet, in Excel 2010, and can be downloaded from the OrganicMaineGarlic website should you want to enter your own figures. The budget will be discussed line by line using the Line # reference in the far left hand column.

First, let me define the terms used by Google Adwords in their search modality so that the discussion below will be clear to you.

- *Impressions* – the number of times your ad is shown to an Internet searcher, meaning someone who keys in one of your keywords and sees one of your box ads.

- *Click throughs* (CT)– the number of times your ad is actually clicked by a searcher, and they are led to the website listed in your box ad.

- *Conversions* – the number of times the searcher takes a desired action upon encountering the landing page on your website, in the case of this example, the purchasing of your product.

You will see from this example that the primary cost you must control is the spending for Google AdWords. If your selling price, click through rate and sales conversion rates are all low you may not be able to afford to advertise via Google Adwords. Google expects you to get at least a 1% click through rate which means at least 100 CT's (click throughs) for every 10,000 impressions. The number of CT's are driven by 1) the quality of your ad (high quality ads usually generate higher percentages of CT's), 2) your daily Google Adwords budget (in this example, $10.00 per day) and 3) the maximum amount you are willing to spend per click through (in our example we vary the Max Budget/CT from $0.10 to $0.25 and finally to $0.50. Since our daily budget is fixed at $10.00 per day, as the price per click through rises the number of CT's that we can afford declines. Basically we will *lose* CT's because our budget is not high enough. Google will tell you that you are not getting all the CT's you could because of these constraints. Eventually you must raise the max rate per click through, raise the maximum daily budget, raise your price, some of each, or quit advertising on Google Adwords and take a different approach.

I will now lead you through the calculations noted on the exhibit below so that you may try the spreadsheet on your own if you desire.

Line #	How to Sell Seed Garlic on the Internet - SampleBudget							
1	Item Selling Price	$80.00						
2	Max Budget / CT >	$0.10	$0.25	$0.50				
3	Impressions	10,000	10,000	10,000				
4	Click Through %	1.0%	1.0%	1.0%				
5	Daily Budget	$10.00	$10.00	$10.00				
6	Potential CT per day	100	100	100				
7	Max CT per Budget	100	40	20				
8	"Lost" CT	0	60	80				
9	Max Budget / CT	$0.10						
10	Max CT Per Day		100	100	100	100	100	100
11	Conversions Percent		1.0%	2.0%	3.0%	4.0%	5.0%	10.0%
12	Units Sold		1	2	3	4	5	10
13	Daily Revenue		$80.00	$160.00	$240.00	$320.00	$400.00	$800.00
14	Monthly revenue	30	$2,400	$4,800	$7,200	$9,600	$12,000	$24,000
15	Google Fee		$300	$300	$300	$300	$300	$300
16	Weebly Fee	3.0%	$2.40	$4.80	$7.20	$9.60	$12.00	$24.00
17	PayPal Fee	2.9%	$2.32	$4.64	$6.96	$9.28	$11.60	$23.20
18	Shipping	$3.50	$105.00	$210.00	$315.00	$420.00	$525.00	$1,050.00
19	Revenue per month		$1,990.28	$4,280.56	$6,570.84	$8,861.12	$11,151.40	$22,602.80
20	Max Budget / CT	$0.25						
21	Max CT Per Day		40	40	40	40	40	40
22	Conversions Percent		1.0%	2.0%	3.0%	4.0%	5.0%	10.0%
23	Units Sold		0.4	0.8	1.2	1.6	2	4
24	Daily Revenue		$32.00	$64.00	$96.00	$128.00	$160.00	$320.00
25	Monthly revenue	30	$960	$1,920	$2,880	$3,840	$4,800	$9,600
26	Google Fee		$300	$300	$300	$300	$300	$300
27	Weebly Fee	3.0%	$0.96	$1.92	$2.88	$3.84	$4.80	$9.60
28	PayPal Fee	2.9%	$0.93	$1.86	$2.78	$3.71	$4.64	$9.28
29	Shipping	$3.50	$42.00	$84.00	$126.00	$168.00	$210.00	$420.00
30	Revenue per month		$616.11	$1,532.22	$2,448.34	$3,364.45	$4,280.56	$8,861.12
31	Max Budget / CT	$0.50						
32	Max CT Per Day		20	20	20	20	20	20
33	Conversions Percent		1.0%	2.0%	3.0%	4.0%	5.0%	10.0%
34	Units Sold		0.2	0.4	0.6	0.8	1	2
35	Daily Revenue		$16.00	$32.00	$48.00	$64.00	$80.00	$160.00
36	Monthly revenue	30	$480	$960	$1,440	$1,920	$2,400	$4,800
37	Google Fee		$300	$300	$300	$300	$300	$300
38	Weebly Fee	3.0%	$14.40	$28.80	$43.20	$57.60	$72.00	$144.00
39	PayPal Fee	2.9%	$13.92	$27.84	$41.76	$55.68	$69.60	$139.20
40	Shipping	$3.50	$21.00	$42.00	$63.00	$84.00	$105.00	$210.00
41	Revenue per month		$130.68	$561.36	$992.04	$1,422.72	$1,853.40	$4,006.80

Line #1 – Item Selling Price – this is set in the example at $80.00 our average price when selling seed garlic.

Line #2 – Max Budget per CT – this ranges from $0.10 to $0.25 to $0.50. Each of these amounts is represented by the exhibits below in Line #'s 9 to #31.

Line #3 - Impressions – The example assumes that your keywords will receive 10,000 impressions per day.

Line #4 – Your keyword click through percent is assumed at 1%. This is the minimum click through rate considered acceptable by Google. You may experience higher or lower rates.

Line #5 Daily Budget – This is fixed at $10.00. In general, regardless of other factors you will find that if your daily budget is fixed at $10.00, you will be paying Google $300 per month for a 30 day month.

Line #7 Max CT per budget – You will see that the most CT's you can achieve will be controlled by how much you are able to spend per day.

Line #8 *Lost CT* – The lost CT's are the number of potential CT's that you could achieve minus those that your budget will permit. Thus if you can spend $10.00 per day and your average cost per CT is $0.25 you will only be able to afford to receive 40 CT's which 60 short of your maximum achievable. Thus your *lost* CT's will equal 60. Google will notify you of this shortfall stating that an increase in your daily budget will lead to more CT's.

Lines #9, 20, and 31 each show the results if your Max Budget per CT ranging from $0.10 to $0.50.

Lines #11, 22, and 33 show a projected Conversion Percent. In this example on Line #11 a Conversion Percent of 1% will yield one unit sold. This means that for every 100 CT's, a one percent conversion rate will yield a sale of one unit. A 2% conversion rate will yield sales of two units, and so forth. 10,000 impressions x 1% CT = 100 CT's x 2% conversions = 2 units sold.

8

. . . .

Summary

So, there you have it. We have shown you how we set up a Weebly e-commerce website, how to get going with Google Adwords, and then wrap up the process with PayPal. We have supplied a spreadsheet to help you understand how the three products interact in terms of dollars spent by you. The spreadsheet may help assess the reality of your e-commerce plans and provide the beginnings of a budget for the process. Should you decide to move ahead, we wish you the best of luck and success with your sales of seed garlic on the Internet.

9

Appendices

Appendix 1.0		
Weebly E-Commerce Export Data Fields		
Seq.	Field Description	Format
1	Order #	10 digits
2	Transaction Date	xx/xx/xxxx
3	Status Shipped	Status
4	Currency	USD
5	Subtotal in $	x.00 -
6	Shipping $	x.00 -
7	Tax Total $	x.00 -
8	Tax Rate	Percent
9	Total $	x.00 -
10	Refunded $	x.00 -
11	Shipping First Name	

12	Shipping Last Name	
13	Shipping Email Address	
14	Shipping Address	
15	Shipping Address Line 2	
16	Shipping Postal Code	
17	Shipping City	
18	Shipping Region (State)	
19	Shipping Country	
20	Shipping Phone	xxx-xxx-xxxx
21	Billing Name	
22	Billing Address	
23	Billing Address 2	
24	Billing Postal Code	
25	Billing City	
26	Billing Region (State)	
27	Billing Country	
28	Product ID	
29	Product SKU	
30	Product Name	
31	Product Options	Delivery date options
32	Product Quantity	
33	Product Price	x.00 -
34	Product Sale Price	x.00 -
35	Product Total Price	x.00 -
36	Product Taxable	Y/N

Appendix 2.0		
PayPal E-Commerce History Export Data Fields		
Seq	Field Description	Format
1	Transaction Date	xx/xx/xxxx
2	Transaction Time	xx:xx:xx
3	Time Zone	PDT
4	Name	First and Last
5	Transaction Type	Shopping Cart Payment Received
		Payment Sent
		Cancelled Fee
		Refund
		Reversal
		Temporary Hold
		Authorization
		PayPal Services
6	Status	Completed
		Partial Refund
		Refunded
		Removed
		Incomplete
7	Gross	$x.00 -
8	Fee	$x.00 -
9	Net	$x.00 -
10	From Email Address	
11	To Email Address	
12	Transaction ID	17 characters
13	Payment Type	Instant
		PayPal balance
14	Counterparty Status	Unregistered

		Verified
15	Address	Confirmed
16	Item Title	Shopping Cart
17	Item ID	Blank
18	Shipping	$x.00 -
19	Insurance	Blank
20	Sales Tax	$x.00 -
21	Option 1	Blank
22	Option 1	Blank
23	Option 2	Blank
24	Option 2	Blank
25	Reference	For cancelled fee, refund, reversal, credit to credit card
26	Invoice number	For postal service fees paid on USPS website
27	Custom Number	Comments input by customer
28	Receipt ID	Number of receipt sent to customer
29	Balance	Cumulative balance in PayPal account for the company
30	Address Line 1	
31	Address Line 2	
32	Town/City	
33	State	
34	Zip	
35	Country	
36	Contact Phone Number	
37	Balance impact	Credit Debit

10

Index

www.ingramcontent.com/pod-product-compliance
Lightning Source LLC
Chambersburg PA
CBHW051417200326
41520CB00023B/7266